Why Have Kids?

Also by Jessica Valenti

Full Frontal Feminism
He's a Stud, She's a Slut
The Purity Myth
Yes Means Yes

Why Have Kids?

A NEW MOM EXPLORES THE TRUTH
ABOUT PARENTING AND HAPPINESS

JESSICA VALENTI

NEW HARVEST
HOUGHTON MIFFLIN HARCOURT
BOSTON • NEW YORK 2012

This edition published by special arrangement with Amazon Publishing

For information about permission to reproduce selections from this book,
write to Permissions, Houghton Mifflin Harcourt Publishing Company,
215 Park Avenue South, New York, New York 10003.

www.hmhbooks.com

Library of Congress Cataloging-in-Publication Data
Valenti, Jessica.
Why have kids? : a new mom explores the truth about parenting and
happiness / Jessica Valenti.
p. cm.
Includes bibliographical references.
ISBN 978-0-547-89261-0
1. Motherhood. 2. Parenthood. 3. Working mothers. 4. Work and family.
I. Title.
HQ759.V277 2012
306.874'3 — dc23
2012022392

Book design by Brian Moore

Printed in the United States of America
DOC 10 9 8 7 6 5 4 3 2 1

For Hilda and Camila—
I will never be able to fully articulate the depth of my gratitude
for the love and care you have shown Layla.
I know she will carry it with her always.

Contents

Introduction

MOST PEOPLE GET FLOWERS when they give birth—I got a two-pound baby and a failing liver. Thanks to a critical bout of preeclampsia, my foray into parenthood was marked with medical urgency rather than congratulations. There were no balloons or cigars passed around, just worried glances and the hum of machines checking vital signs.

When I went in for a routine exam during my twenty-eighth week of pregnancy, I felt fine. The look on my doctor's face when she took my blood pressure for the third time, however, made it clear that I was far from the healthy, glowing pregnant woman I imagined myself to be. Even after I was admitted to the hospital a mere ten minutes later, my husband and I figured it was all a fluke. After all, I didn't feel sick, and we had months to go before our daughter was due.

But within two days, my liver was in danger of failing from a second pregnancy complication called HELLP syndrome, and I was rushed in for an emergency C-section. It was twenty-four hours before I was well enough to see my daughter, Layla, and almost a week before I could touch or hold her. She spent eight weeks in the hospital, over which time she endured more medical invasiveness than most adults could bear. During that time, we held it together—mostly because we had to.

Once the immediate danger was over—when my husband and I knew that Layla would be fine—that's when my real trouble began. I was incredibly grateful to have my daughter and my health, but I couldn't stop mourning the pregnancy and childbirth I thought I was going to have. I desperately wanted the entrance into parenthood that I expected, the one I had planned so carefully for.

Just two days before I was hospitalized I had been leisurely touring St. Luke's-Roosevelt Hospital wondering what kind of birth experience I wanted. I was torn between the birth center—relaxation tubs and bragging rights on giving birth "naturally"—or a hospital room, where there were sweet, sweet epidurals. It never occurred to me that I wouldn't be able to choose what circumstances my daughter would be born under, and it certainly never crossed my mind that I could end up with a sick baby.

Later, I was thrown another parenting curveball when I didn't feel the sense of all-encompassing joy and love for Layla that friends and family told me would come. (One friend told me that the welling of love she had for her son felt almost like an emotional orgasm.) When a colleague asked me over lunch what new-mom emotion I found most surprising, I had to admit that it was ambivalence. Now, the frightening events surrounding Layla's birth certainly influenced how I felt about my daughter—I was too afraid to feel the incredible love I had for Layla because I still feared losing her—but as the months went by, I was able to compartmentalize the post-traumatic stress and sadness I felt about how my daughter came into the world.

This feeling was something else. Something that no baby book or words of wisdom prepared me for. It wasn't unhappiness so much as an unsettling sense of dissatisfaction, an itch of emptiness that was accompanied with overwhelming shame for not feeling "completed" by parenthood. This was not what I expected.

NO EXPECTATIONS

Parenting needs a paradigm shift, plain and simple. The American dream of parenthood—the ideal that we're taught to seek and live out—doesn't come close to matching the reality, and that disconnect is making us miserable.

Fewer than 5 percent of American families employ a nanny.[1] Most parents don't spend over five hundred dollars on a stroller, or use cloth diapers. Hell, most mothers don't even breastfeed for longer than a few months,[2] despite all of the hoopla over breast being best. What is being presented to us as the standard of parenting—through books, magazines, and online media—is really the exception. The truth is much more thorny, and not nearly as glamorous.

Americans are desperate to figure out why, exactly, they are so dissatisfied and anxious over parenthood. They seek advice from every Tiger Mother or *bebe*-raiser to help with their parenting woes. But looking to other cultures—or, more accurately, generalizations about other cultures—is a fruitless search for a quick fix.

American parenting is too complex to lead one to believe

that a brutal schedule of piano lessons or a croissant will magically erase the nuances and troubles that go along with raising children. Parental leave policies are woefully inadequate—if not nonexistent—at most American workplaces, and many mothers worry about losing their jobs or being forced onto the "mommy track" once their child is born. Parents are paying exorbitant amounts of money for child care, and feeling guilty to boot about dropping their kids off. Social expectations about what constitutes a good or a bad mother haunt every decision, and the rise of the parental advice industry ensures that moms and dads feel inadequate at every turn. Our children bring us joy (most of the time) but the parenting hurdles—whether systemic or personal—are still there, unchanging.

Parents can no longer smile pretty, pretending that the guilt, expectations, pressure, and everyday difficulties of raising children don't exist or that the issues that plague so many American families can be explained away in a how-to guide.

Fifty years ago, Betty Friedan wrote the groundbreaking book *The Feminine Mystique* about "the problem that has no name"—the everyday domestic drudgery that made a generation of women miserable. Today that problem has a name (and quite often, poopy diapers). The problem isn't our children themselves; it's the expectation of perfection, or, at the very least, overwhelming happiness. The seductive lie that parenting will fulfill our lives blinds Americans to the reality of having kids.

Now, there's nothing that can *truly* prepare people for the reality of parenthood, but most Americans don't like uncertainty. (Hence all the parenting guides, magazines, and advice gurus!)

People spend so much time planning for children—tracking ovulation, undergoing IVF, picking out nursery colors, and creating birth plans—that we expect very specific outcomes.

Women expect to get pregnant relatively easily (despite scare tactic headlines warning any woman with a solitary gray hair that she's more likely to be hit by lightning than conceive—like ABC's 2010 story that warned women who want kids, "The Sooner the Better: 90 Percent of Eggs Gone by Age 30"[3]); they expect to have a healthy baby, to breastfeed without complications, that their significant others will pick up half the slack, and that children will fill them with a happiness so pure that they'll be content staring at their wee faces for hours without regard for life, limb, or bathroom breaks. The expectations are too high for reality to ever measure up.

The nameless problem Friedan explored was one that resonated with many, but not all women. She was speaking to a particular group of American women—the Betty Drapers, privileged middle-class homemakers. To those like my mother and grandmother—who worked at factories and in bars—the oppression of homebound cookie baking sounded pretty damn sweet. Today's parenthood problem isn't so exclusive; it affects us across class, gender, and race. I suppose some people do live in that world of perfect parenting, where the worst of times are the trials and tribulations associated with finding the perfect stroller or a bottle that has the best internal-vent system to prevent milk aeration and "nipple collapse." Some parents are lucky enough to have the time, energy, and money to think over what preschool will make their kid most likely to go to Harvard or what parenting "style" will make their child the most secure.

But this world is imaginary for most Americans, even if it

is positioned as the norm and propped up as the ideal. Parenting is hard—really hard. And I don't mean run-of-the-mill difficulties that everyone knows parents face—the sleep deprivation and the loss of freedom, for example. I'm talking about the soul-crushing drudgery of day-to-day parenthood that we're too embarrassed to talk about. The boredom, the stress, the nagging dissatisfaction, and the sense of personal failure that parents feel when raising a kid isn't all it's cracked up to be. Perhaps worst of all is the guilt that so many women buy into because they're too ashamed to admit that despite the love they have for their kids, child rearing can be a tedious and thankless undertaking.

Over the last twenty years, that shame and guilt has become central to modern motherhood. And why not? Parents—women especially—are reminded every day how they don't measure up. If mothers work outside the home, they're forcing their kids into early puberty[4] and turning them into bullies[5] by sending them to day care. If they stay at home with their kids, they're over-parenting feminist sellouts with no life. There's a multimillion-dollar industry built on the notion that parents are clueless. Where would Dr. Spock or Dr. Sears be if mothers didn't feel somehow inadequate? And if it's not the media and books, it's the constant one-upmanship between mothers that keeps parents in their place. Are you breastfeeding? Co-sleeping? Baby-wearing? In *Bossypants,* Tina Fey calls them "teat nazis"—"a solely Western upper-middle-class phenomenon occurring when highly ambitious women experience deprivation from outside modes of achievement. Their highest infestation pockets are in Brooklyn and Hollywood."

The social pressure alone is enough to send women running scared to the closest IUD. No matter how much American parents put into caring for their children, there is always someone there to let them know that it is just short of acceptable.

Social pressures aside, the everyday obstacles are there as well. Women, in particular, have more than a "nameless" reason to be unhappy. Financially, they're screwed. The wage gap that American women are all too familiar with before they have children only widens once they become mothers—even more so if they're single mothers, or not white. A study from the University of New Mexico showed that mothers earn up to 14 percent less than women who don't have children. A Cornell University study showed that a child-free woman is twice as likely to be hired as a mother with an identical résumé, and is offered about eleven thousand dollars more in starting salary. And of course, the United States is the only industrialized nation without paid maternity leave, and some families pay half their income toward child care.

At home it's not any better. When women become mothers, they are more likely to report unhappiness in their marriage[6]—in large part because of the unequal division of housework once the baby arrives. Even marriages that were once egalitarian will skew toward the traditional once couples become parents. When you get a husband, you also get seven extra hours of housework a week (whereas when men get married, they lose an hour of housework), and mothers do on average eighteen more hours a week of housework than fathers. Utopian visions of equal parenting give way to diaper duty, late-night feedings, and breast pumping. (If you've ever had the misfortune of using one of these contraptions, you know that the repetitive nipple pulling that leaves you feeling like a dairy cow would make anyone depressed.)

The truth is that women have plenty of reasons to be unhappy. But what has surprised me most as I researched this book (and as a parenting newbie) is that women *know* many of the reasons they're dissatisfied. We kvetch on online forums about husbands who don't do their share at home, or we commiserate with coworkers over the lack of reasonable maternity leave or flextime. We regularly discuss the everyday problems that make parenting harder. But instead of addressing this dissatisfaction head-on and trying to fix it, too many American parents are resigned to believing that this is just the way it is.

Thanks to the Internet, however, moms are speaking up more than ever. The simmering anxiety that Judith Warner outlined so well in her 2005 book *Perfect Madness* is now boiling over into a parenting frenzy—but the outrage seems to end at the personal, leaving the political aside. Mommy blogs organize to take down diaper ads but are largely silent on the lack of paid maternity leave. They'll complain about unfair division of labor at home yet rarely link their husband's dirty laundry to the larger political system that tells women they're better suited for housework. One woman who wrote in to a local email list for mothers was almost embarrassed as she asked how other moms got their husbands to "help" with the baby.

The constantly evolving way that raising children has been perceived in our culture is, in part, why Americans are unable to articulate the problem with parenting.

It used to be that parenting was thought of as a community exercise, with help from family and neighbors (whatever happened to "It takes a village"?); now it's positioned as all-American individualism. Erica Jong, in a *Wall Street Journal* column on motherhood, said if "there are other care givers, they are invisible . . . mother and father are presumed to be able to do this alone."[7]

When one women's organization was considering starting a child care program in 2002, for example, it ran focus
groups of mothers to find out what they thought of the lack
of affordable care. Overwhelmingly, the sentiment was pride-
ful: *Why should the government help with child care when my
kid is my responsibility?* I've heard similar arguments from parents who don't vaccinate their children— *Yes, it may put the
community in jeopardy, but I'm going to do what's best for my
child.* Or mothers and fathers who are willing (and able) to
pay a great deal of money for their child's education, rather
than fight to improve the system— *Who cares about the sepa-
rate-but-equal educational system so long as my son goes to a good
school?* It goes on and on—in our quest for perfect parenthood, we've lost all sense of community.

The rise of individualism doesn't stop there, but has also
impacted the way Americans view marriage. Today, for the
most part, people don't get married out of duty or tradition;
they get married for love. Kate Bolick in *The Atlantic's* "All
the Single Ladies" calls it "a post-Boomer ideology that values emotional fulfillment above all else."[8] And now, Americans parent for love, too. Gone are the days of reproducing to
have an extra pair of hands at the farm or family store. Parents
expect their children to be their soul mates in the same way
they expect of their spouse—they want children to make their
lives and families complete.

When these sweet little beings who are supposed to be the
center of parents' universe don't manage to fulfill their lives
completely, we come back to the most overwhelming sentiment of mothers across America: guilt. If our kids are our
world, how could we be so heartless as to hate the drudgery
that comes along with them?

American parents love their children. But it's not enough to say that the sacrifices are worth it because of how great your kids are. If the love that people have for their children were enough, then why do 20 percent of new mothers experience depression? Why do some parents abandon or abuse their children? If having children is the best and most wonderful thing we have ever done, then how do we explain to our bundles of joy that a third of them were unplanned?

Perhaps it's the fear of the big problems—the nightmare scenarios no one wants to ever think about—that keeps us so preoccupied with the upper-middle-class minutiae of parenting and ignoring the bigger issues. Better to obsess about what preschool your child will go to or whether or not their food is organic and homemade than to worry about the much more serious and terrifying realities of having a child.

We're scared to death thanks to the media—telling us about strollers that will slice your kids' finger off, or ad campaigns likening co-sleeping to letting your baby sleep in bed with a butcher knife. But the reality is that American kids are more likely to go without health insurance than be kidnapped. They're more likely to get a serious illness than be abused by a child care worker or left in a hot car. We focus on the absurd, rather than the everyday, because the mundane is too real—too out of control—to face.

After all, having a critically ill baby never crossed my mind—even though one in six babies in the United States is born prematurely. I was much more concerned about finding baby clothes that weren't so girly as to offend my feminist sensibilities and buying fashionable nursing shirts. Even though early on in my pregnancy I had an amniocentesis after a blood test showed that Layla might have a genetic disorder (she didn't), it still never entered my mind that I would get anything but a big, fat healthy baby. I was naive, yes, but, like most parents, I was just being self-protective. Because like it or not, becoming a parent *is* a life-and-death situation. And the terrifying reality is that from the moment our children are born there's always a chance they could be taken away from us. I don't know about you, but worrying about BPA-free pacifiers seems a hell of a lot more sanity saving.

This is a book about how the American ideal of parenting doesn't match the reality of our lives, and how that incompatibility is hurting parents and children. Because the expectation of a certain kind of parenthood—one where we're perfect mothers who have perfect partners, where our biggest worry is whether or not to use cloth diapers—makes the real thing much more difficult to bear.

We have to get real about our expectations. Children don't exist to make us happy, and treating them as such will just make them—and us—miserable. But if we can manage to beat back the guilt and sense of personal failure that so many women buy into—and feel no shame when we admit that child rearing can be a tedious and thankless undertaking, despite the love we feel for our kids—then we can start to take on the broader social and political issues that are really what chip away at the joy of parenting.

This book will likely make you angry. It's meant to. These topics are controversial and close to home: a recipe for defensiveness if there ever was one. There are certain American parenting trends that I take issue with because of my personal beliefs and politics—my take might make you feel insulted. That's okay. All parents—including myself—should be challenged to think more critically about their choices and the

way they impact their children, their lives, and the rest of society. No one likes the "mommy wars" or endless battles over
what kind of parent is best, but debating these issues vociferously just means that they matter to us. That we care about
parenting, and that we care about our kids. What could be
more important to fight over and to fight for?

LIES

ONE

Children Make You Happy

My husband and I are either going to buy a
dog or have a child. We can't decide whether
to ruin the carpet or ruin our lives.

— *Comedian Rita Rudner*

WHETHER OR NOT we have kids, are planning to
have kids, are married, single, or are still kids ourselves, the baseline assumption about every one of
us is that one day we'll be parents. If you're a woman, this belief is likely to follow you your entire life.

In 2006, *The Washington Post* coined the term "pre-pregnant"[1] in response to a report from the Centers for Disease
Control[2] recommending that all women of childbearing age
care for their pre-conception health. The agency wanted all
American women—from the time they have their first period
until they go through menopause—to take folic acid supplements, not smoke, not "misuse" alcohol, maintain a healthy
weight, refrain from drug use, and avoid "high risk sexual behavior." The CDC was asking women to behave as if they

were already pregnant even if they had no intention of con-
ceiving in the near—or far—future. For the first time ever,
a U.S. government institution was explicitly saying what social norms had always hinted at: That all women, regardless of
whether or not they have or want children, are simply moms-
in-waiting.

Telling women that what is best for their pregnancies is
automatically best for them sets up a dynamic in which motherhood—from the very beginning—is defined as the woman
prioritizing the needs of her child over her own.

The idea that women should stay healthy not for their
own well-being but to make their uteruses hospitable, did not
go over well with many women. Rebecca Kukla, a professor of
internal medicine and philosophy at University of South Florida and author of *Mass Hysteria: Medicine, Culture, and Mothers' Bodies*, says, "Do lesbians, women who are carefully con-
tracepting and not interested in having children, 13 year olds,
women done having kids, really want their bodies seen as prenatal, understood solely in terms of reproductive function?"

Kukla tells me she knew she wanted to research the culture of motherhood and pregnancy after she became pregnant
herself, ten years ago. "I got so taken with the experience, I
couldn't help but write about it." Her watershed moment
came when she was reading *What to Expect When You're Expecting*. At the beginning of each chapter, the book had a picture called, "What you may look like." It was a drawing of a
transparent torso—no head, arms, or legs—with a fetus in-
side of it. Readers were meant to figure out if their baby bump
was around the right size.

Kukla says she stared at the picture while looking in the
mirror at her own pregnant belly, trying to figure out if her

body looked "right." If her bump was too small, it could mean her fetus wasn't growing properly. If it was too big, it meant she was fat.

"All of a sudden I realized, wait . . . I have a head and arms—I don't look like this at all!"

Kukla says that this obsession with pregnancy that largely erases women—sometimes literally, as in the case with *What to Expect*—from the picture has meant that intensive parenting has essentially "extended backwards" through pregnancy, and even prior to conception. "It literally treats the non-pregnant body as on its way to pregnancy."

The preconception movement has historical roots, Kukla notes, in the desire to have women produce perfect citizens— the state has always had a stake in ensuring that pregnant women's bodies were monitored. But what critics of the preconception movement, like Kukla, find so disturbing is the way in which medical professionals today are selling this as care for women.

"They were specifically targeting low-income women and women who were vulnerable or marginalized that they thought wouldn't be able to get into the clinic for preconception care since they weren't interested in being pregnant—so they packaged it as whole woman care."

A "preconception checklist" from the March of Dimes[3] includes questions like "Do you see a dentist regularly?" and "Do you eat three meals a day?" One letter from the California Preconception Care Initiative to doctors says that, "One of the best times to integrate preconception care into primary care is during a visit that includes a negative pregnancy test . . . because this is a time when many women learn how easily an unintended pregnancy can occur." There's a very *The*

Handmaid's Tale quality to this kind of questioning—a disturbing standard of women's bodies being treated as potential incubators at all times.

Since the medical establishment does not trust women to know if and when they want to become mothers, it goes without saying that it does not believe a woman is capable of making informed decisions *if* she does indeed choose pregnancy. The truth is that science shows women *can* have wine when pregnant, or the occasional stinky cheese. (A 2010 British study, for example, found no negative effects in five-year-olds whose mothers drank lightly during pregnancy.[4]) It's the abuse of substances that have a negative impact on a pregnant woman and a fetus—but the medical industry doesn't trust women enough to make that distinction.

And when fetal health—or potential fetal health—is centered in medical care, women's own care could suffer. Kukla tells me that when she was thirty-seven, after she had her first and only child, she went to the doctor to get an antibiotic for a urinary tract infection. Her doctor asked her if she might be pregnant. She said no. He asked if she might become pregnant; she said no again. He asked if she was sexually active. "He wouldn't drop it," Kukla said. Her doctor said he wouldn't prescribe her the antibiotic he would usually give out since there was a chance she could become pregnant; instead he insisted on a less popular, weaker drug that would cause fewer complications during pregnancy.

"Never mind that I'm a grown woman who is capable of using birth control and would have ended a pregnancy had I become pregnant. Because I presented as someone that could become pregnant, I got this other, less-effective drug."

This obsession with parenthood as a given, and women as mothers-in-waiting, reveals something central about American parenthood. We don't have a choice. Parenting is simply something everyone—women especially—is supposed to do. Since such a huge decision is seen as inevitable, and not a decision at all, it makes sense that everything related to parenthood becomes a question, a choice, an all-important decision to be fretted over.

ANXIOUS PARENTHOOD

American parenthood is fraught with anxiety, uncertainty, and unhappiness—it starts before birth, before pregnancy, before putting your ovulation schedule on a calendar and figuring out the best time to have sex, before the glimmer of sexual attraction toward that handsome man next to you on the plane. From the time we're born, really, we're taught what it is to be a good parent. When we're children, our parents are the center of our world, and we mimic their love (or neglect) accordingly.

As we get older, we worry about what career choice will mesh best with a family—if we're lucky enough to be able to choose our job. We think about our age. We worry about what kind of partner we'll have. If we'll be able to have children "naturally." We fret over what we'll eat during pregnancy, if we can exercise, do that yoga pose, eat that stinky cheese. We wonder if the birth of our children will go smoothly, if we'll have a water birth, a natural birth, a planned C-section.

Even if we don't want children, the idea of parenthood as inevitable is everywhere. A *Today* show segment asked, "Is it wrong for a woman not to want to have children?" Doctors refuse to perform tubal ligations on women who are considered "too young" (this being largely a problem for white upper-middle-class women—poor women and women of color are routinely offered or pressured to have long-term birth control or sterilization). Twenty-five-year-old Lauren, who always knew she wouldn't have children, had to go see four doctors before she found one that would perform the procedure. "They were all nervous I would change my mind later," she said.

For those who aren't sure if they want children, there's very little room for error or space for conversation and consideration. Your chances of getting pregnant each month when you're thirty years old is about 20 percent, by the time you're forty years old your chances have plummeted to 5 percent. You have six months to try before most medical associations will recommend that you see an infertility specialist. Women who would like to spend time weighing their options are told they don't have the luxury.

If you are lucky enough to get pregnant the old-fashioned way, you still have plenty to agonize over. Here are some complications that the Mayo Clinic reports are more common in pregnant women over thirty-five: gestational diabetes, high blood pressure, chromosomal abnormalities in the fetus (such as Down syndrome), and miscarriage. You're also at greater risk for endometriosis, blocked fallopian tubes, fibroids, ectopic pregnancy, a C-section due to problems like placenta previa (in which the placenta blocks the cervix), and—horrifyingly enough given all of these other worries—having a stillbirth. But don't worry, ladies, it's not just you. Men can also have a decline in fertility in their late thirties, and some studies say that kids born to men over forty have a higher chance of having autism. Yay, equality?

The science is sound; there's no doubt that it's harder to have kids the older you get—but the panic by which this information is relayed to American women borders on the maniacal. When Sylvia Ann Hewlett's book *Creating a Life: Professional Women and the Quest for Children*—which warned women that the older and more successful they became, the less likely they were to have kids—was released in 2002, for example, it was to headlines such as, "The Baby Panic," "The Late Great Egg Hunt," "The Loneliness of the High Powered Woman," "Working Against the Clock," and "The Feminists' Big Lie." In the United Kingdom, the book was even retitled *Baby Hunger*. It was the modernized version of the eventually debunked *Newsweek* story that claimed women over forty were more likely to be killed by a terrorist than to find a husband. Today, you can just look at how tabloids froth at the mouth over the supposedly sad state of affairs of Jennifer Aniston's empty uterus.

But it's once we're actually pregnant—after we've managed to jump through the incredible hoops to make ourselves such—when real trouble begins. Not only do we have to keep to those CDC guidelines—like not smoking or drinking, and taking supplements—but we also have to look to the thousands of books, websites, and brochures that tell us exactly what we can and cannot do. Mostly, it's "cannot." Books like the best-selling *What to Expect When You're Expecting* (now being made into a feature film whose movie posters feature a pregnant Cameron Diaz and the quote, "If I knew I'd have a rack like this, I would've gotten knocked up years ago!") list in meticulous detail the various dangers that a pregnant woman should watch out for, from sushi to hot baths. Websites like BabyCenter feature forums where women across the country can ask one another—and experts—whether or not their behavior is somehow putting their pregnancy at risk.

Here are some of the questions women have asked in online forums about their pregnancies:

Can I paint? Work out?

Is it safe to have sex doggie style?

Can I get manicure/tattoo/perm/hair-color?

Am I allowed to do sit-ups?

Can I use the microwave?

Should I not lift my suitcase to the overhead compart-
ment when I'm on a plane?

Should I do sit-ups?

Can I use my laptop?

Will an orgasm hurt the baby?

Can I sleep on my stomach/side/back/a waterbed?

Can I take a plane across the country?

Can I go on rides at the amusement park?

Is it safe to drink tap water/soda/coffee/Kombucha?

Can I take sleeping pills/anti-depressants/Xanax?

Should my pee be this color?

What pregnant women *can* do is a much smaller, and much more regulated, list. The sample "pregnancy diet" in *What to Expect When You're Expecting,* for example, requires a PhD in math and nutrition to keep up with.

The book tells women they should eat 350 more calories a day than normal during their second trimester and 500 extra calories in the third trimester. (For those of us unfamiliar with counting calories, this is already a daunting task.) The "diet" requires women to have three daily servings (or 75 grams) of protein and three servings of Vitamin C, which could take the form of 1/8 of a honeydew melon, 1/4 of a papaya, or 1/2 of a medium mango. You need four servings of calcium — *What to Expect* recommends 1/4 cup of grated cheese, a cup of yogurt, or 1 ounce of cheese. Then there are four servings of leafy or yellow vegetables or fruit, two servings of non-yellow fruit and veggies, six daily servings of whole grains and legumes, and at least one thing from their "iron rich" list, which includes sardines, buffalo, and blackstrap molasses. Oh yeah, and four servings of fats and at least eight 8-ounce glasses of fluid every day. No big deal.

When I was pregnant, there were days at a time when I would eat only apples and scrambled eggs. (Ask my poor husband about the time I asked for a new glass of water because the one he brought me smelled funny. "Water doesn't have a smell!" he yelled before storming off to get me a new glass.) As anyone who has ever had insane pregnancy hormones surging through their body knows, there is no possible way to keep to a "diet." Though as long as you manage to stay away from the pregnancy diet evils, such as unpasteurized cheese and wine, you should escape without too much judgment.

Once you make it through your pregnancy, however, a whole new heap of judgment awaits you in the delivery room.

My mother is an amazing parent by any standard. She breastfed my sister and me. She had her own business that she shared with my father (a women's clothing store), which meant she could stay home when she wanted to and bring us to work when she wanted to. She was there for everything: sporting events, school plays, recitals, bedtime stories, skinned knees, and—as we got older—heartbreak, acting out, and leaving home. The only child care help she had was my grandmother and the occasional older cousin to babysit. But if you ask my mom, this bastion of maternal intuition and self-sacrifice, she'll tell you that she has always felt a little less than a complete mother. Why? Because she had a C-section.

It's not just if, how, and when we get pregnant, or how we "behave" during that pregnancy, but even the way we choose to bring children into the world has become a marker of what kind of parents we'll be. Are we a "natural" mom or are we "too posh to push"? Did we even *try* to go without drugs?

When (or if) we do have kids, we not only have to worry about keeping them entertained, stimulated, educated, and happy at all times, but we have to relay to the world around us that parenting is the best decision we ever made, no matter how hard or draining it is. Even if we're running on two hours of sleep, if our nipples are raw from using a breast pump, or if we haven't been able to urinate without a child looking on in over two years, we smile through it, assuring our child-free friends that not only is it worth it but that we're happier than we've ever been in our lives. The truth, of course, is very different. Given the worry, the hoops, and the constraints we face before we've even gotten to the nitty-gritty of learning to live with our children, is it any wonder than American parents are unhappier than ever before?

My own experience with parental unhappiness was largely rooted in the fact that my daughter was born prematurely, in the middle of a medical crisis that threatened my life. Still reeling from the trauma of delivering my daughter almost three months before my due date and recovering from a complicated C-section, my first "parental" actions were comprised of giving the limited energy I had to a hospital-grade breast pump, which made me feel like an electronically milked cow, and visiting Layla's incubator (just to look, since I wasn't able to touch her right away). Those were literally the only things I could do as a mother.

Fifty-six long days later, when Layla finally came home, I froze. Crippled by fear and post-traumatic stress, I remained at a distance. Yes, I fed her and bathed her and held her—but it was all cursory, done without joy. It wasn't that I didn't love Layla, I was just unable to feel the immense love I had for her because of my overwhelming fear that she would die. Though I still feel incredibly guilty for those first months of unhappiness and non-engagement, I can pin what happened on a trauma. I have an excuse. I can't imagine what my guilt would be like if I didn't, if I was simply unhappy for no "good" reason.

SMILING, HAPPY PEOPLE

Nearly every study done in the last ten years on parental happiness shows a marked decline in the life satisfaction of those with kids. A 2011 study published in *Psychological Science* from scientists at the University of Waterloo, for example, showed that parents routinely exaggerate their parental joy as a way of justifying (self-soothing, perhaps?) the incredible economic cost of having children. As many as 20 percent of new mothers experience symptoms of depression, and a study of five thousand families from the Center for Pediatric Research at Eastern Virginia Medical School showed that one in ten fathers also meet the standards for postpartum depression.[5] Another eight-year study of over two hundred couples published in the *Journal of Personality and Social Psychology* showed that 90 percent reported a decrease in marital satisfaction after having a baby. And that's the good news.

If you're poor and lack social and family support, you're more likely to be unhappy in your marriage after having children and depression skyrockets to over 50 percent for women.[6] If you're a stay-at-home mom, you're more likely to experience depression; but if you're a working mom who has unrealistic expectations about your ability to balance work and family responsibilities, your chances for unhappiness and depression also go up. And these studies don't even touch on the ennui, the feeling that this could not possibly be *it,* all that parenthood is cracked up to be.

This isn't to say that parents don't love their kids or find joy in raising them. Of course we do. It's an incredible, unparalleled experience. But we also tend to add a happy gloss over our lives as parents because to discuss the hardships is considered whiny, ungrateful, or—in some circles where parenting has become a competition—as losing. We put on a brave face and make jokes about the sleepless nights, the lack of sex, and the baby puke smell that is now in all of our good shirts.

Because after all, the expectation of happiness is why we've had kids. When researchers for a 2010 Pew study asked parents why they decided to have their first child, nearly 90 percent answered, for "the joy of having children." For the happiness that comes with loving and raising another human being. When that happiness doesn't pan out, it's difficult to admit—not only because it seems ungrateful, but because to tell the truth seems like an insult to the children that parents love so much.

But maybe kids aren't supposed to make us happy. Historically, Americans had children to help with the family farm or to have an extra set of hands around the house—to produce members of a larger community. Today, parenthood has become less about raising productive citizens than it is about creating someone to love us unconditionally, someone on which to focus all of our energy and love. The enormity of that expectation not only leaves unhappy parents wondering why they're not swooning over their children, but it is also creating a generation of young people who think the world revolves around them. (After all, they're just kids—that's an awful lot of pressure to put on such tiny humans.)

According to the researchers at University at Waterloo,

when children had more economic value—when they were working at the family store instead of racking up private school costs or draining our pockets for diaper money—parents were much less sentimental about them. As the economic costs of children have gone up, so has the notion that parenthood is joyful, fulfilling, and emotionally rewarding. Parental joy is largely a new—but powerful—idea.

Daniel Gilbert, psychology professor at Harvard University and author of *Stumbling on Happiness*, says that parents are often surprised to hear that they'd likely be happier and more satisfied with their daily life if they didn't have children. "They value and love their children above all things—how can my children not be a great source of happiness?"

Gilbert says it's not so much that children don't make you happy—they do bring joy into people's lives—it's that kids also "crowd out" other sources of happiness.

"So people have a first child, often find in the first year or two that they're not doing many of the other things that used to make them happy. They don't go to the movies or the theater. They don't go out with their friends. They don't make love with their spouse. All the things that used to be sources of happiness are no longer there."[7]

But just because parental joy isn't necessarily a given—or because it can be a dangerous expectation—doesn't mean we can't strive for it. Or that we can't put an end to all of the things that are making us miserable. The truth is, we should try to get happy for our sake and for our children's sake. Kids who have depressed parents are interacted with less than their counterparts with happy, non-depressed parents; kids of dads with depression have smaller vocabularies at two years old than kids of non-depressed dads. We owe it to our kids—and to the kids who aren't ours—to ask questions about why parenthood is so hard, what we can do to make it an easier, happier endeavor, and what we're lacking to ensure that happens.

Sometimes the unhappiness is a hurdle of our own invention—the enormous expectations that we place on our children to bring us joy, or the extreme guilt and judgment we heap upon ourselves if we don't parent in some exacting "correct" way. Often the obstacles to parental happiness are structural—there's a reason that parents who have more resources and more financial security are happier than their counterparts with lower incomes. Most of the time, however, it's a combination of the two—our desires and our limited resources—and, most damaging, the belief that there's nothing we can do to change things.

The truth is that parental joy is within our grasp—it just requires a little knowledge, some work, and the desire to shift the status quo.

TWO

Women Are the Natural Parent

[E]ven brief maternal separations can be psychologically
damaging to young children, and that from the
young child's viewpoint no one, not even Dad, can
substitute for Mom. . . . In a child's eyes, Mother
is not merely absent; she is gone forever.

— *Natural Family Living: The Mothering Magazine Guide to Parenting*

I F YOU'VE NEVER seen an eight pound baby grunting
over the toilet, I assure you it's a sight to behold. Videos
of mothers holding their infants over their laps or directly
over the toilet as they go in the potty litter mom-sites and
YouTube.

These babies aren't toilet prodigies—if only there were
such a thing! Some have been using the toilet since they were
just weeks old thanks to their parent's adherence to "elimination communication," a practice more akin to a parenting
style than toilet training.

Proponents of EC—also called "diaper freedom" or Natural Infant Hygiene—claim that babies, from birth, simply
don't need diapers. The basic tenet of EC is that if parents

take the time to read their babies' facial cues and body language, they will know exactly when their children need to "eliminate" and can take them to the bathroom—holding them over the toilet or balancing them on their own open legs so their infant can do their business unfettered by a diaper. Parents are also encouraged to hiss in their child's ear—it's a sound the baby will come to associate with going to the bathroom so that parents can elicit a sort of Pavlovian response (though they would never describe it as such) from their children.

EC acolytes also believe that diapers impede babies' communication with their parents, interfere with their bodies' natural rhythms and needs, and that by not practicing EC, parents are neglecting their children on a very fundamental level. Christine Gross-Loh, author of *The Diaper-Free Baby: The Natural Toilet Training Alternative,* writes that "by ignoring a baby's elimination signals, we're asking her to tune out a natural instinct and instead endure something she likely finds unpleasant." (Clearly Gross-Loh has never seen the joyful face of a baby who happily plays blocks while sitting in her own poop.)

If EC sounds like a lot of work, that's because it is. Infants can urinate as often as every fifteen minutes, making those runs to the bathroom the central part of an EC mom's day. Add to that the fact that EC doesn't allow parents to ever be very far from their children—after all, you need to be studying your baby's face, watching for telltale signs of an oncoming elimination—and a mother who practices EC is essentially spending every minute of every day attending to her child's bodily functions.

But Gross-Loh pooh-poohs, excuse the pun, the notion that women don't have the time to sit vigil watching for elimination signals. She writes that "many parents are in close proximity to their newborn babies" anyway. (Moms in this scenario all have maternity leave or unlimited resources to ensure that they're home with their children.) For those whose children are older and have become mobile, while there are "challenges," Gross-Loh assures that EC parents will be so "in tune" with their children that they will just know when they need to eliminate, even if they're in a different room. "That is the nature of the awareness you cultivate during this journey," Gross-Loh writes.

To EC diehards, like Krista Cornish Scott, who chronicles her adventures in diaper-free living on her website Free to EC!, this has nothing to do with the amount of work it takes. To her, EC is about the basic human desire to communicate with your child. Scott says that any parent who pays attention knows that babies tell us when they need to use the bathroom. Just think of those cute grunty-baby faces!

"Once you accept the idea that babies are aware of this need [to use the bathroom], how can a parent who wishes to fulfill their child's basic and primal needs continue to ignore elimination communication?" Scott believes that parents who scoff at EC are simply not interested in caring for their children to the same degree that she is. When parents teach their children to use diapers, Scott says, "you are telling them that the need not to soil themselves will not be met." (In an interview with an Australian television show[1] on attachment parenting, Scott also called strollers and bouncers "neglectomatics," something that parents "just put the baby in . . . to forget about them.")

Now, for obvious reasons, EC is not a mainstream practice. Only a handful of books have been written on the subject, several thousand members populate an online message board, and its celebrity spokesperson is Mayim Bialik, former star of the nineties sitcom *Blossom*—a "holistic mom" advocate who once said of babies who can't survive a home labor that perhaps "it is not favored evolutionarily." So yes, not mainstream by any stretch of the imagination.

Though elimination communication is radical, it tells a disturbing story of modern mothering. Perhaps no other parenting philosophy so fully epitomizes the overwhelming pressure on mothers to be everything to their children, as well as the obsession in American culture with venerating a particular kind of mother—one who gives up everything for her child.

Women almost exclusively do the tedious work of EC. The practice assumes that all women have the time—the idea that women work outside the home is hardly ever addressed—and desire to devote themselves entirely to the minutia of their children's lives and bowel movements. It suggests that women who don't follow this intense regimen aren't connecting with their children, and, most dangerous of all, it frames the subsuming of one's own desires into that of their children as somehow "natural" and better than women having distinct and separate needs. In short, it's a feminist's worst nightmare.

Much like current parenting trends that capture the media's attention—right now it's "natural mothering," everything from home births to baby-wearing—EC also represents the white middle-class phenomenon of fetishizing a largely imaginary "third world" motherhood that's supposedly more pure and natural than Western parenting practices. A common refrain from EC advocates, for example, is that mothers in India and Africa don't use or need diapers. Never mind that there isn't a monolithic "Indian" or "African" parenting experience (or that Africa isn't a country), or that the mothers they're referring to could be very happy to have diapers, were they available. It's easy to appropriate a condescending fixation on "underdeveloped" motherhood when you have the financial means and leisure time to pick whatever kind of parenting works for you at the moment. This clueless racism is captured perfectly on Krista Cornish Scott's website, where she assures readers that "EC is not just for African bush-women."

No matter how privileged the perspective, though, this return to a supposedly simpler, more "maternal" kind of parenting is being touted as the new feminist and feminine ideal. Or, more accurately, a return to the natural moms we were always meant to be.

In the last decade the "natural parenting" movement has spiked: Home births in the United States have increased by 29 percent since 2004,[2] there are over one million blogs dedicated to natural and Attachment Parenting, and parents are increasingly home-schooling their children. The idea of natural parenting has become so mainstream that gossip magazines run stories like, "Celebrity Moms: Who Had Natural vs. C-Section Births?" and ask which celebs were "too posh to push."

But if one kind of parenting is "natural," what does that make all other kinds of child rearing? Despite all of the empowered rhetoric around the new maternal ideal—women's intuition! maternal instinct!—isn't this just a spiffed up version of telling women that their most important role in life is a domestic one?

ATTACHED AT THE SLING

When I was pregnant, Dr. William Sears's book—given to me by a friend who had a perfect home birth, damn her—was my bible. I read *The Baby Book: Everything You Need to Know*

About Your Baby from Birth to Age Two every night, highlight-
ing passages for my husband to check out and nodding my
head in agreement over the emphasis on parent-child bonding. (Dr. Sears is the modern guru of Attachment Parenting—the popular philosophy that encourages mothers to stay
in close physical proximity to their babies at all times, usually entailing baby-wearing, breastfeeding, and co-sleeping.)
I imagined myself writing articles while wearing Layla in a
sling, cooking up organic baby food during my lunch hour,
and breastfeeding while lounging happily in bed, occasionally
dozing off with the baby.

Some of these things happened—I can puree up a decent
organic meal and I managed to use cloth diapers for a month,
before the stench from the laundry bin became too much to
bear and the inconvenience of finding covers small enough
to fit Layla proved too much for my already worn-thin patience—but when I wasn't able to fulfill all of my natural
mama plans, I was disappointed (in myself most of all). At
first I thought it was because of the emergent nature of Layla's
birth—that the stress of having a child under less-than-per-
fect circumstances made it difficult to do my maternal best.
Now I know better.

If you have any sort of life independent of your child,
flexibility is the only thing that will get you through the day.
There's simply no way you can take care of your own needs
if you—and only you—take care of your child's every need.
And while natural maternal instincts may kick in for some
people, they're not necessarily the norm.

I had a moment once that I thought was natural maternal
bliss. Layla, who didn't take easily to breastfeeding because of
her prematurity, was happily suckling away for the first time
in weeks. I was looking down at her being nourished from my

body, my eyes welling up. This was the moment I had heard about, the moment I was waiting for. The thought had no sooner crossed my mind when Layla sneezed, leaving a gigantic green-and-red booger stuck to the tip of my nipple. I realized then that there was no book or philosophy that would prepare me for parenthood. Despite my fantasy of a Dr. Sears-approved motherhood, reality hit me square in the tit.

Petra Büskens,[3] a Netherlands-based motherhood researcher who is currently working on a book about mothering and psychoanalysis, says that this myth of an intuitive natural motherhood is actually an ideal constructed by modern economic and political realities. It used to be that mothers had a community of support—they parented with other women, men, and children and did so while doing non-domestic work in addition to parenting. But as women were pushed out of the public sphere, social changes "elevated motherhood to the status of a divine occupation" and told women that their mothering should become a solitary, domestic endeavor.

Thirty-three-year-old Danielle, who lives in a suburb of Boston, has this very problem. Danielle had her first child when she was living a four-and-half-hour drive away from her family and close friends in New York.

While the idea of Attachment Parenting her son appealed to Danielle, it was near impossible given the fact that she worked. "I literally straddled a toilet bowl pumping breast milk in a public restroom because I had to travel for work, but at four months postpartum I was still pumping fifteen ounces of milk every day." She says the lack of social support along with all of the work she was doing to "naturally" bond with her son made her feel like she was going crazy.

"My son is doing great even with all the challenges I faced, but I'm fairly certain he'll never feel the brunt of how hard it's been. Me, however, well . . . I've very nearly lost my mind through all of it."

Büskens writes, "The expectation is far from the reality of modern parenting—there is nothing 'traditional' about this." She notes that the "debilitating" guilt that mothers often feel is due to adhering to a supposedly natural philosophy of parenting without having any of the support their great-great-foremothers had.

"Mothers are attempting to carry out rigorous schedules of attached mothering in an increasingly fragmented and unsupportive social context." Essentially, we're Attachment Parenting without a net.

When Andie Fox, thirty-nine, became a mother, one of the things she noticed right away was the tension between her and her partner in terms of equality. "When I was in the early stages of being a mother, I was preoccupied with fairness," she tells me.

"It was the shock of seeing our relationship become more and more traditional." So Andie did what a lot of moms do today: She started a blog. She writes at Blue Milk[4] about the intersection of mothering and feminism. She also blogs quite a bit about Attachment Parenting, which, after looking for what parenting "style" she had, seemed to match up quite nicely with what she was already doing and feeling.

She says as much as she identifies with Attachment Parenting, however, she wishes that some of the books or experts behind the practice would acknowledge the way that women are expected to shoulder so much of the parenting responsibility.

"Attachment Parenting has been less than transparent about the inequality that happens very naturally—and maybe has to happen—in those early stages of parenting an infant.

Even if they had acknowledged that if you breastfeed, you're the source of everything, it might make it a lot easier."

Feminism, she says, hasn't always been entirely helpful for mothers either—particularly in terms of being able to identify and articulate the desire around choosing to parent and becoming a mother. But she thinks that if Attachment Parenting started to openly discuss the ways in which women are expected to be primary caregivers, that more feminist-minded women would be open to the practice and wouldn't be so surprised when they experienced the shock of doing so much of the parenting work themselves in those first months.

For Andie Fox, APing her children—inequalities and all—has felt like the thing that has worked for her most naturally.

Büskens points out, though, that it's incorrect to call this kind of parenting "natural" when the philosophy of care has been introduced into Western motherhood through the deliberate marketing of books and experts that is then put into action by mothers in "isolated nuclear families."

And indeed, the Attachment Parenting of Dr. Sears is more parental advice empire than holistic consciousness-raising group. His *Baby Book* has sold over two million copies, and its twentieth anniversary edition is due out in 2013. The original Dr. Sears—William Sears—is now just one of multiple Dr. Searses that you can look to for advice. The Sears sons, Jim, Bob, and Peter, have all become doctors and are part of the family business, doling out advice on the AskDrSears.com website and making the media rounds. Dr. Jim Sears is even a regular on the CBS show *The Doctors*.

Dr. Sears's three daughters—Hayden, Lauren, and Erin—are not involved with the AP empire—apparently it's only men who are qualified to give mothering advice. Sears's wife Martha, an RN who calls herself a "professional mother," is also featured on the website and in Sears's books, but her advice is often featured as an aside. (It's a bit disconcerting, this feminist must say, to see the homepage list the photos and names of the clan—Dr. Sears and his sons all get full salutations while his wife is listed simply as "Martha.")

The Sears family also has a full product line, Dr. Sears Family Essentials ("Healthy products you can trust, from our family to yours!"), which includes everything from vitamin supplements and snacks to drinks and baby wipes. AP moms can buy Dr. Sears-approved baby flatware, diaper cream, and even baby slings (a mere sixty dollars for a swath of cloth!). And of course, you can choose from over fifteen books—from the mainstay *Baby Book* to *Dr. Sears' LEAN Kids* and *The A.D.D. Book*. The Dr. Sears flock also shills for the dietary supplements Juice Plus, a company that the Better Business Bureau accused of running misleading ads claiming their "gummies" were a viable alternative to fruits and vegetables. Not exactly the back-to-basics version of motherhood that Sears touts in his books.

Despite the corporate disconnect, mothers are APing their kids by the hundreds of thousands. It's something feminist author Erica Jong called "an orgy of motherphilia" in a 2010 *Wall Street Journal* article.[5] Jong scoffed at Attachment Parenting, arguing "you wear your baby, sleep with her and attune yourself totally to her needs. How you do this and also earn the money to keep her is rarely discussed." Jong wrote that Attachment Parenting—along with environmental PC-ness that drives moms to make their own organic baby food and seek out all things green—"has encouraged female victimization" and traps mothers.

Some accused Jong of oversimplifying this form of parenting, while others suggested that she was simply trying to make excuses for her own lackadaisical parenting history. Katie Allison Granju and Jillian St. Charles wrote in *The New York Times* blog Motherlode that "Jong should quit blaming mothers for the things the feminist movement has yet left undone,"[6] and that "many women will tell you that becoming a mother was the most politically radicalizing experience of their lives."

Jong's own daughter—Molly Jong-Fast—even weighed in, writing that Jong "was famous, always touring, always working, always trying to cling to *The New York Times* bestseller list. Famous people, who are often intensely driven workaholics, are typically not focused on their children. To my mother . . . children were the death of a dream; they were the death of one's ambition."[7] (But, she noted, Jong did get her a pony.)

Call-outs like Erica Jong's are often met with this kind of derision and skepticism—not to mention the attacks on one's mothering bona fides. It's much the same backlash that French feminist Elisabeth Badinter received in the wake of her best-selling book *The Conflict: How Modern Motherhood Undermines the Status of Women.* Hell hath no fury like La Leche League scorned—Badinter's argument that formula, diapers, and jarred baby food were all "stages in liberation of women" has left natural-mothering proponents foaming at the mouth.

The largely unspoken critique of Attachment Parenting, however, is that for mothers who aren't upper middle class, it's something that they do without calling it a philosophy or adhering to a certain set of rules. Tedra, for example, had her son sleep in her bed and she wore him quite often. But she never read "that damn Sears book because it sounded bossy and annoying."

And for moms who don't have time and resources to put a name to their parenting, the brouhaha over AP seems a bit trite. Mothers who worry about having enough food to feed their children don't necessarily kvetch on online forums over whether or not you should wear your baby. Some parents co-sleep not because they think it will promote the right kind of bonding but because they have only one bedroom—and maybe no crib.

The backlash against this type of criticism may be in part a reasonable defensiveness—who wouldn't get a bit riled if someone attacked how you parent your child? And it's true that arguments like Jong's and Badinter's are polemical and meant to provoke. But our discomfort with theories that take on "natural" motherhood may be more than just self-righteousness; it's self-delusion as well.

Whether you call it Attachment Parenting, natural parenting, or simple maternal instincts, this false "return" to traditional parenting is just a more explicit and deliberate version of the often unnamed parenting gender divide. Whether you're wearing your baby or not, whether you're using cloth diapers or teaching your four-week-old to use the toilet: it's still women who are doing the bulk of child care, no matter what the parenting philosophy. Putting a fancy name to the fact that we're still doing all the goddamn work doesn't make it any less sexist or unfair.

One of the major reasons women—new mothers especially—report being unhappy in their marriages is because of the unequal division of work in the home, including child care. In fact, even marriages in which the partners describe themselves as equals will start to become more "traditional" once a baby enters the picture. All of a sudden the shared responsibilities give way to mother-knows-best essen-

tialism—because the argument implicit in "natural" parenting is that it's women who should be embracing this return to
the instinctive maternal. We're the moms, after all.

When women are the one-and-only for their child, men
not only have a free pass not to participate, but women also
are left to feel like they are somehow bad mothers if they're
not able to go it alone. In a culture that suggests you should
be attached at the hip (literally) to your baby, it should come
as no surprise that moms feel overwhelmed.

Andie believes, however, that the inequity that happens
when natural parenting reigns supreme doesn't necessarily
mean that Attachment Parenting and likeminded philoso-
phies should be discounted off the bat. She says that APing
fits in with feminist ideals in many ways, especially in that
it's "supposed to be a style of parenting that allows women to
perform parenting in their everyday lives."

"If babies are breastfed and carried around and sleep in
bed with you, then in theory they're very portable and that's
certainly been my experience. You can cart them about with
you while you attend to other children or socialize or read a
journal for work or stay overnight somewhere," she tells me.

The problem, she says, is that our institutions are "too
rigid" to allow this kind of incorporation of parenting into
other roles in our lives. And in that, Andie has an indisputable point. Parenting and caretaking are only as oppressive as
our society makes them—and if workplaces and American
culture mores didn't marginalize women and mothering, perhaps the inequality of traditional roles wouldn't be so jarring.

THREE

Breast Is Best

As for your baby, breastfeeding is what he's born to expect. One mother pointed out that it's as if bottles fill his stomach, but breastfeeding fills his soul.

— *The Womanly Art of Breastfeeding, La Leche League*

WHEN ROBIN MARTY GAVE birth to her second child at Unity Hospital in Fridley, Minnesota, she immediately taped a sign to her son's bassinet that read, ABSOLUTELY NO FORMULA. She didn't want any bottle-happy nurses to disrupt Sebastian's breastfeeding regimen while he was in the nursery. Robin even debated whether to give him a pacifier, lest he develop nipple-confusion. This time, she told herself, she was going to do it right.

Robin, thirty-two, grew up in Omaha, Nebraska, and met her husband, Steve, after she moved to Minneapolis. Much to the horror of their Catholic families, they "lived in sin," as Robin put it, for five years. So when Steve proposed, they got married just three weeks later.

"When I was in my twenties, I wasn't even sure if I wanted kids. So it's funny, I'm surprised, at how gooey I've become as a mother."

Robin had her first child, a daughter named Violet, in 2007. She spent two days (yes, *days*) in labor before having an emergency C-section. As a result of the surgery, both Robin and Violet developed severe bacterial infections—Violet was so ill that she had to spend over a week in the Neonatal Intensive Care Unit. Robin had planned to exclusively breastfeed. "Everyone tells you you're going to breastfeed, that's just what you do—it's the natural thing to do and any woman can do it," she says.

But the circumstances around Violet's birth seemed to make that goal impossible. Robin's infection made her tired all the time and pumping became even more difficult. And while Robin was resting in her room, NICU nurses would often give her daughter formula instead of waking Robin. Once Violet came home, Robin tried to nurse, but her milk had failed to fully come in.

"I felt like if you're not able to breastfeed it's because you're doing something wrong. And with Violet, everything that could have gone wrong did go wrong." Robin wasn't going to let the same thing happen again with her son.

So when she got pregnant a second time, she decided she would do everything in her power to breastfeed exclusively. "I put the sign up, and I sat up all night with him at my breast just sucking away. Everyone told me how great I was doing." For the three days that Robin stayed in the hospital, her nurses continually complimented her on Sebastian's latch and how long he was nursing—over ninety minutes every two hours.

When Sebastian lost weight, Robin didn't fret; she knew that babies born by C-section often lost weight in the first few days. By the time Robin left the hospital, her son had dropped from 7 pounds, 8 ounces to 6 pounds, 10 ounces. Her pediatrician recommended supplementing with formula, but Robin refused—instead she called her lactation consultant who encouraged her to continue to only breastfeed. So she kept at it, and Sebastian continued to breastfeed vigorously.

Two days later, at a home-care follow-up, Sebastian had lost another two ounces; he hadn't had a bowel movement in four days. But, again, Robin was told not to worry—as long as he was having wet diapers he was all right. "But I didn't know how much of a wet diaper they meant. He didn't look or act dehydrated, and he was eating all the time," she says.

A week later Sebastian's weight had dropped to under six pounds. The discoloration in his diapers that Robin had chalked up to normal newborn stuff turned out to be crystals in his urine—her son was severely dehydrated and in acute danger. Sebastian was starving. "I assumed that as long as he was always at the breast, he would eventually get enough food because everyone can breastfeed. But I was one of the women who couldn't do it."

After Robin hurriedly started supplementing breastfeeding with formula, Sebastian was back to his birth weight within a week. "I felt like a total failure. I did everything I could," she says. Robin had done everything right this time, and still she wasn't able to make breastfeeding work.

Today, Robin is pregnant for a third time—"It was a surprise!"—and isn't planning on breastfeeding at all. For her, it goes beyond remembering the exhausting pumping sessions with her daughter or even Sebastian's close call. "I know that my body can't do it. There's no reason to try to do it just to prove a point."

When Robin wrote about her experience on an online mothering community, she was eviscerated. She was told that it wasn't the lack of milk that almost starved her son, but doctors and hospital administration that weren't sufficiently supportive or knowledgeable about breastfeeding. Before I spoke with Robin, I noticed that at the end of her post about Sebastian there was an editor's note:

> Here is a response from writer Robin Marty to inquiries she has received. "I was not compensated for writing this post . . . Although I have received the standard Similac offers, coupons and free formula all new mothers have the option to opt in to, I have had no other contact with Similac or any other formula company or marketing firm."

When I asked Robin about the note, she told me that she was bombarded with comments and emails accusing her of being paid by formula companies to write about her experience. "I understand that it's important to talk up breastfeeding because it's good for children, but we have to stop bashing women over the heads with guilt over formula feeding."

But still, Robin says she feels at peace with the decision not to breastfeed her third child. "It's more important that your child is happy and nurtured than that they're fed with breast milk."

Besides, Robin points out, she thought breastfeeding was supposed to be empowering. But now she feels that the pressure around nursing is a way "to tie a woman to the child and the home."

"Supposedly breastfeeding is freeing—you don't have to

worry about the bottles and being out carrying around formula, but there are all these rules that keep you at home and completely tethered to your baby," Robin tells me.

"Almost anything and everything can sabotage the breastfeeding relationship, you're told—giving them a pacifier, supplementing with formula, letting them sleep in a different room, leaving the house. It's all just too much and we're not supposed to talk about it."

PUMP IT UP

That overwhelming "too much" feeling is what led me to stop breastfeeding as well. Though, truth be told, I never made a conscious decision to stop breastfeeding entirely—admitting that I was a total failure in this regard was too difficult. Instead, I stopped pumping—a decision that led to the slow weaning of my daughter.

At first, like Robin, I was intent on breastfeeding; the idea of formula even touching Layla's lips made me nauseated and anxious, as if formula would poison her. (An idea that some breastfeeding proponents suggest quite readily.) But because of Layla's prematurity, I couldn't breastfeed at first—she was too small and her digestive system wasn't fully formed, nor did she know how to suck, swallow, and breathe all at the same time. I would have to wait until she was almost ready to leave the hospital. So instead of breastfeeding, my only "job" while Layla spent two months in the NICU was to pump. And pump. And pump. At least eight times a day—preferably ten times—for fifteen minutes on each breast. That's five hours a day.

At the time, I thought of my breast pump both fondly (Wow, thanks for all the milk!) and simultaneously hated it intensely. It was a reminder of my daughter's preemie status, yet another machine that would replace the "natural" bond that we were missing out on. That, and it hurt like hell.

But for the most part, I was grateful. I was desperate to do something tangible for Layla while she was hospitalized—sitting vigil by her incubator made me feel helpless—and pumping five hours a day was sure-as-shit tangible. But once you face the harsh reality of the pump, no matter how much good you know it will do for your kid, well . . . let's just say there's really no getting over seeing your nipples stretched out four inches longer than they're supposed to be, as they're vacuumed into the pump. (And thanks to the sadistic inventor of the breast pump, the pump part is transparent, so you get to see every inch of the taffy that your former nipple has become.)

My pump, which came in a jaunty little nylon purse that looked like a 1990s Kate Spade knockoff, made a rhythmic sound when operating that sounded a little too much like House music for my comfort. There's something about a club kid beat set to your breasts being tortured that makes the whole ridiculous scenario feel even crueler. And despite the Vaseline-like cream I put on after every pump, my nipples still bled and cracked. It got so bad after a few weeks that I just sobbed and screamed in pain throughout the sessions. But still, I didn't stop—and every time I looked at Layla's drawer in the NICU freezer stacked to the top with frozen breast milk, I felt like it was all worth it. Sure, I was depressed, in pain, and exhausted all the time, but I was doing right by my kid.

Then something miraculous—and devastating—happened. Layla's digestive system was suddenly working full speed. At first, Layla would take only two or three milliliters of milk an hour through her feeding tube. An hour after feeding her, the nurse would check how much she actually digested by sucking out her stomach contents through the same tube—the milk often sat there, undigested. After six weeks, however, she was digesting like a champ. Enough that the IV vitamins and nutrients she had been getting were removed, and she was sustained solely by breast milk. Within a week my freezer drawer started to dwindle. Despite the hundreds of hours I spent pumping, it turned out my supply wasn't as terrific as I thought. Soon I was rushing back and forth to the hospital to make sure they had enough milk. The first day that there wasn't breast milk for Layla, and the nurses used formula, I sobbed. I was devastated, ashamed that I couldn't give my daughter the one "natural" thing I could provide while she was hooked up to so many wires and tubes. But still I kept trying. I gave her as much milk as I could and tried not to think about the formula.

When Layla was able to come home, it didn't get much better. She was able to latch on for short periods of time, but because we were desperately trying to get her to gain weight, I was still pumping to increase my supply and so we could measure out exactly how much milk she was getting.

I made an appointment with a lactation consultant that a friend recommended. She was warm and understanding, if a bit hippieish for my taste—she refused to use hand sanitizer before touching Layla, saying it wasn't environmentally friendly. I was a bit aghast—sanitizer was like a religion in our household—but perfect, I thought, I need someone "natural" to help me! Leigh Anne had plenty of suggestions: My pump wasn't powerful enough (?!), I should be taking herbal supplements, drinking oatmeal shakes several times a day, and trying "power pumping"—going at it *every* hour. I felt overwhelmed, but was happy to have some pointers. When I mentioned that I was supplementing with formula, she wasn't as horrified as I imagined a lactation consultant would be, though she did gently recommend using donor milk—another woman's breast milk. I balked.

Instead, I just tried harder. After a particularly hard night in which I screamed for almost a half hour straight while pumping, my husband suggested I quit. I was so obsessed with giving Layla breast milk that I wasn't bonding with her at all—I was too busy at the pump, and too miserable. It took me a long time to realize that what Layla needed more than breast milk was a mother who wasn't exhausted and stewing in shame.

After I stopped breastfeeding entirely, I remembered Betty Friedan writing in *The Feminine Mystique* about a mother who suffered a nervous breakdown when she couldn't breastfeed. That seemed about right. Our ability to nurse is presented to American women as the most basic, natural thing a woman can do for her child. So when it doesn't work—or, shame on us, we simply don't want to do it—we're blamed for being selfish, or not trying hard enough. That's a message that's hard not to internalize.

I must admit that I once looked down a bit on mothers who chose not to breastfeed; I didn't understand why they wouldn't at least try. After all, everyone tells us it is the best thing we can do for our babies. But what if it's not? What if all the guilt and shame and bleeding nipples are all for something that's not as amazing for our children as we've been led to believe?

Dr. Joan Wolf, Texas A&M professor and author of *Is Breast Best? Taking on the Breastfeeding Experts and the New High Stakes of Motherhood,* has been called bitter, a "looney," even a supporter of child abuse for asking this very question.

Wolf speaks slowly and deliberately when she's discussing her work. "I've been called all kinds of names. One person said my argument was tantamount to denying the Holocaust," Wolf told me. Apparently, if you want to incur the wrath of mothers across America, you need only to suggest that breastfeeding isn't all it's made out to be.

It's commonly accepted that breastfeeding is superior to formula feeding; everyone from the National Institutes of Health to the American Academy of Pediatrics says it's the best option for babies. It's why I let my nipples bleed and why Robin almost inadvertently starved her son—we never questioned the notion that breast milk was nutritionally better, or that breastfeeding would bond us to our children, increase their immunity, even make them smarter.

But Wolf says the science doesn't support the dogma around nursing. "I never doubted that breastfeeding had myriad health benefits, so I was actually very surprised at what I found in the medical literature," she said.

What Wolf found boils down to this: While thousands of studies show that breastfed babies are healthier on average than formula-fed babies, none of this research has shown that it's actually the breastfeeding that leads to better health. Moms who have the time and support to exclusively breastfeed—remember my five-hour-a-day pumping sessions?—may be more likely and able to support their children's health in other ways. Women who have jobs where employers let them disappear every couple of hours to pump may have more money and better health insurance than mothers who work in jobs where there is no break, let alone a break room to pump in. Mothers who stay at home or have long maternity leaves are similarly privileged. And nearly every study that has looked at the benefits of breastfeeding has failed to take issues such as these into account.

The only real benefit that has been proven to be a direct result of breast milk, Wolf said, is that babies who are nursed have fewer gastrointestinal issues. But higher IQs? Increased immunity? Not so much.

So why all the hype? Almost every medical association agrees that breast is best, Michelle Obama has touted breast-feeding as part of her fight against childhood obesity, and the U.S. surgeon general has put out a "Call to Action to Support Breastfeeding," with tips for moms, health care providers, and employers on how to make nursing easier for new mothers. Pro-breastfeeding campaigns in New York State even try to convince moms to nurse by touting how well it helps new mothers lose weight.

Wolf sees the overblown benefits as part of a broader cultural issue, something she calls "total motherhood"—the notion that mothers should be experts in everything having to do with their children (from health issues to consumer safety)—which she describes as a "moral code in which mothers are exhorted to optimize every aspect of children's lives, beginning in the womb." This total obsession with one's children to the detriment of one's emotional and psychological well-being—captured flawlessly in Judith Warner's *Perfect Madness*—goes way beyond the breast. It starts with not eating sushi and stinky cheeses when pregnant, then breastfeeding at all costs, and as children get older, making sure they're constantly "stimulated." It's never-ending. (This impossible

standard that mandates women be consumed by motherhood, putting all of their "selfish" needs aside for the good of
the baby, never takes into account, however, that what's best
for mother might just be beneficial for baby.)

Not surprisingly, the reception of Wolf's book and her
idea of total motherhood have been mostly confrontational.
When she made an appearance on the popular daytime "medical" show *The Doctors,* for example, Wolf was raked over the
coals by the well-coiffed panel of celebrity MDs.

Toward the end of her segment, after each and every doctor scoffed at the idea that breastfeeding isn't best, Dr. Wendy
Walsh said, "Breastfeeding mothers are different mothers;
women who are breastfeeding actually relate to their children
more empathetically and compassionately." (And those who
don't nurse don't emotionally relate to their children?) Dr.
Walsh ended Wolf's interview by saying, "I just want to re-
mind you that when a woman has a baby, that is her. That is
her happiness. Giving to your baby is giving to yourself." Total motherhood, indeed.

The social message is clear: If breastfeeding is what "com-
passionate," "good" mothers do, then women who don't
breastfeed are bad. Hardly mothers at all, really. And this message isn't just coming from talk show hosts or government
campaigns—when it comes to judging women for not breastfeeding, it's other mothers who are the worst offenders.

I'm not sure what would make some breastfeeding advocates so adamant that there's only one right way to feed a
baby. It's one thing to believe breastfeeding is best and parent accordingly, it's quite another to tell other mothers that
they're somehow subpar.

I'll never forget one of the first times I had Layla out with
me by myself (I was nervous about bringing her out into the

germ-infested world). I was at a café several blocks away from my house, having an espresso and feeling pretty good about how well my daughter was doing. After a few minutes, Layla started fussing so I gave her a bottle. Another mother, sitting a few tables away from me with her toddler son, called over, "You know, breast really is best. If you need help nursing, let me know." I was in shock. For whatever reason, this person, this stranger, found it completely appropriate to comment on the way I fed my daughter — maybe she was a bit clueless, perhaps she felt some sort of overly familiar relationship because we were both mothers. Or maybe she was just kind of an asshole. In any case, I was horrified and ashamed. (The anger would come later.)

And I'm certainly not the only one. Dozens of mothers I spoke to have similar stories. For one, it was the constant check-ins by her mother-in-law who continually tried to be "helpful" by suggesting different ways she could nurse even after she knew her daughter-in-law had chosen to formula feed. For thirty-three-year-old Sara, who went on medication after being diagnosed with severe postpartum depression, it was a neighborhood mothers' group who didn't understand why she couldn't just forgo antidepressants.

This isn't to say that moms who breastfeed don't get their fair share of harassment. Moms across the United States have organized "nurse-ins," when department stores or restaurants have kicked out breastfeeding moms. In Kansas, moms can even carry around a laminated card that they can whip out to demonstrate their legal right to breastfeed in public spaces.

But there's something about mothers who don't breastfeed that gets our judgmental hackles up. For example, while researching this book, I quoted an article on my blog about a hospital in the United Kingdom that was going to stop making free formula available for new mothers—I disagreed with the decision. Thanks to what followed, I got quite an education about the politics of online mothering and pro-breastfeeding blogs.

Within minutes, a blogger called FeministBreeder started messaging me; in her Twitter description she touts herself as a "rocker chick turned natural mom" (I'm dying to know what kind of mother isn't a "natural" one). She suggested that my quote was "harmful to women's health," that I hadn't researched the issue, and that I was "siding with the formula marketing industry" who takes advantage of "vulnerable" women. One woman likened formula feeding to smoking, while another wrote that giving your child formula was akin to giving them McDonald's. An actor, Somali Rose, wrote to me that women who don't breastfeed are just worried about their breasts sagging and denying their natural purpose in life: "Why does being a feminist have to mean denying what you're body was designed to do? I don't care if my boobs sag I'm breastfeeding."

But the most telling message came from Laura Castle in Las Vegas, who wrote, "Breastfeeding has been the most challenging, and at times the most grueling, thing I have ever done in my life! But the same way I chose to become a mother. I am choosing to make that sacrifice. Anything less is not option. Being a mother is all about sacrifice and if you aren't willing to make those sacrifices for the health and well-being of your child, then maybe you should think twice about becoming a mother."

So if you don't want to breastfeed—if you're not prepared to "sacrifice"—then you simply shouldn't have children.

You're depressed and exhausted? Come on, you just need to sacrifice a little more! You have never-ending breast infections? Suck it up and get your ass to a La Leche League meeting! (Oh, you have to work? That's too bad.) Your baby is premature and the stress of the NICU has left you with almost no milk? Just take this vitamin, drink this oatmeal shake, and pump your breasts for five hours a day! You don't have a job that has a pump room or refrigerator? Well, what's more important—your job or feeding your child? (Someone actually said this to me once.) You don't have the time or physical and mental energy to do this? Sorry, but this is the natural way—better that you're ready to jump out a window than give your baby formula.

Obviously I support breastfeeding. We need mandated paid maternity leave, insurance that pays for lactation consultants and breast pumps, employers who are required to have a space and breaks for pumping moms, hospital- and state-funded breastfeeding support groups, and more. But formula feeding your child is just as valid and healthy a choice as breastfeeding—and sometimes, as in my and Robin's case, it's the best choice there is.

FOUR

Children Need Their Parents

We've internalized the notion of rugged individualism
so deeply that we believe we are solely responsible for
our children's health and well-being. And we believe
that this belief, instead of being a sign of hubris or of
despair, is an entirely normal and natural thing. This
leads us to place terrible pressure upon ourselves—and
gets our society almost entirely off the hook as far
as responsibility for children and families goes.

— *Judith Warner*

N 2011, *The New York Times*[1] reported an odd bit of information about the U.S. Census Bureau and a regular report they release called, "Who's Minding the Kids?"[2] It
turns out that for the purposes of synthesizing the statistics
for this particular report, the Census Bureau assumes that
the mother is the "designated parent," which means that anyone who takes care of the child besides the mother counts as
"child care"—including dad.

In 2010, fathers were caring for their children 32 percent
of the time. But to the government this work didn't count as

parenting; it was child care. The message couldn't be clearer: Mom parents, Dad babysits.

Lynda Laughlin of the Census Bureau's Fertility and Family Statistics Branch told KJ Dell'Antonia, *The New York Times* blogger who broke the story, "Regardless of how much families have changed over the last fifty years, women are still primarily responsible for work in the home. . . . We try to look at child care as more of a form of work support." When Dell'Antonia asked Laughlin if the Census Bureau collected statistics on how much time women spend giving "work support" to their husbands, she replied, "We don't report it in that direction."

Fifty years of feminist progress later, and women are still thought to be the default parent. (Even as evidenced by the name of the *NYT* "parenting" blog that reported this news—it's called Motherlode.)

It's no wonder, then, that decades after the second wave of feminism, the argument over how best to care for children still almost entirely falls on women's shoulders. Men aren't simply excused from the conversation, they're actively excluded by a culture and politics that still promote the idea that the only appropriate caregiver, the only natural parent, is the mother.

Even in the so-called mommy wars between working mothers and stay-at-home mothers, the underlying value system is one that assumes having professional help to raise our children—be it subsidized day care or a live-in nanny—is a necessary evil, something women do because the best possible option isn't available. After all, even working mothers would like more time with their children—that's why they fight for flextime and better maternity leave and pay. Americans believe that the best option for children is parents as caregiv-

ers, period. The days of "it takes a village" are gone—because
even if taking care of our children does require the help of
other people, parents are likely to feel badly about it rather
than seeing it as a natural part of raising a child as part of a
community.

Americans believe it's best for kids to be with their parents
as much as possible; the truth is, however, that our kids do
better when they have a lot of people invested in their growth
and development—not just their parents, and not just their
mothers.

Deborah Lowe Vandell, professor and chair of the Department of Education at the University of California, Ir-
vine, tracked over thirteen hundred children who were studied from the time they were one month old until their teen
years. The study measured the type of day care, the quality
of the care, and the number of hours children attended. Vandell and her colleagues found that more than 40 percent of
the children were given high-quality care, and that 90 percent
of them spent some time in the care of someone other than
their parents before they were four years old. The results of
Vandell's long-running study, published in 2010 with the National Institutes of Health, showed that children in high-quality child care scored higher on academic and cognitive tests
as teenagers than children who didn't attend child care. They
were also less likely to have behavioral issues than children
who attended lower-quality child care centers.

The key, of course, is having *high-quality* child care. In
2005, Georgetown University psychology professor Deborah
Phillips studied students in Tulsa, Oklahoma, to research the
impact of preschool on children. Oklahoma preschool teachers have to have at least a bachelor's degree, classes are limited

to ten students per teacher, and the caregivers are paid on the same scale as public school teachers across the state. Phillips's study looked at two groups of children of the same age—one comprised of children who had gone to preschool and one group that had not. In three different cognitive tests—spelling, word identification, and applied problems—the children who had been to preschool did substantially better than those who hadn't. These cognitive differences held true across race and socioeconomic status.

DO IT FOR THE COUNTRY

Despite the sound research, Americans, culturally, still see day care as a less-than-ideal option. The notion that parents—women in particular—should be in charge of their children's development and care started around the time of the American Revolution. Women were encouraged to uphold the ideals of patriotism by instilling republican values into their children. It was how women were expected to contribute to the nation; it was part of their civic duty. "Republican Motherhood" marked the first time in American history that the domestic sphere was seen not just as separate from the public sphere but as having value and importance to the nation. This ideal of motherhood was not just one that told women they needed to care for their kids; it was also up to them to teach them and pass on American values. It made mothers' roles much more important, and gave American women good reason to be educated—for the good of taking care of their children.

Linda Kerber, a professor of U.S. women's history at the University of Iowa, has written that the Republican Mother "was a device which attempted to integrate domesticity and politics."[3] She continues:

> The Republican mother's life was dedicated to the service of civic virtue; she educated her sons for it; she condemned and corrected her husband's lapses from it. . . . The creation of virtuous citizens was dependent on the presence of wives and mothers who were well informed, "properly methodical," and free of "invidious and rancorous passions." As one commencement speaker put it, "Liberty is never sure, 'till Virtue reigns triumphant. . . . While you [women] thus keep our country virtuous, you maintain its independence." Virtue in a woman seemed to require another theater for its display. To that end, the theorists created a mother who had a political purpose, and argued that *her domestic behavior had a direct political function in the republic.*

Women's behavior in the private sphere had a direct impact on the nation and its politics, therefore when women gained more power in the public sphere, it was bound to shake up the way motherhood was thought of.

Today we can trace this distrust or uncertainty around child care to an intense societal fear that erupted when American women entered the workforce en masse. (There were always mothers who worked, of course, but it wasn't until white middle-class and upper-middle-class moms took to job seeking that the American public became worried.) This shift was particularly dramatic for married women with children; in 1950 only 12 percent worked. By 1980 that number was 45 percent, and in 2002, 61 percent. And according to the Department of Labor,[4] women in the workforce have doubled over the last fifty years. Today, over 58 percent of the labor force—those who are working or looking for work—are women.

This influx of women into the workplace was largely thanks to feminist efforts—from the 1963 Equal Pay Act, which made wage discrimination illegal, to the 1968 ruling of the Equal Employment Opportunity Commission (EEOC) that sex-segregated help-wanted ads were illegal. Not everyone, however, was pleased by the progress women were making in the public sphere—particularly because it meant fewer women at home caring for children.

DO IT FOR THE CHILDREN

Susan Faludi, in her groundbreaking book *Backlash: The Undeclared War Against American Women,* quoted a top military official in the 1980s who said, "American mothers who work and send their children to faceless centers rather than stay home to take care of them are weakening the moral fiber of the nation." It seems Republican Motherhood hadn't left the building.

The media backlash that Faludi recorded was just as bad as the political:

> In 1984, a *Newsweek* feature warned of an "epidemic" of child abuse in child care facilities, based on allegations against directors at a few day care centers—the most celebrated of which were later found innocent in the courts. Just in case the threat had slipped women's minds, two weeks later *Newsweek* was busy once more, demanding "What Price Day Care?" in a cover story. The cover picture featured a frightened, saucer-eyed child sucking his thumb. By way of edifying contrast, the eight-page treatment inside showcased a Good Mother—under the title "At Home By Choice."

Panicked statistics and reports—despite their sketchy veracity or the way they were deliberately misconstrued by the media—abounded, claiming that day care could irreparably damage your children who would lose the all-important mother-child bond, get sicker more than kids of stay-at-home moms, and be more depressed and emotionally damaged. A controversial 1988 report, for example, "The 'Effects' of Infant Day Care Reconsidered," by developmental psychologist Jay Belsky,[5] then at Pennsylvania State University, purported to show that infants who had more than twenty hours a week of "nonmaternal care" were at risk for psychological and behavioral problems. Nonmaternal care was defined as just that—any care, be it nanny, babysitter, dad, or day care. Belsky wrote that children who were deprived of this much maternal care would have "insecure attachment," which could lead to "heightened aggressiveness, noncompliance, and withdrawal in the preschool and early school years." In his report, Belsky added caveats and qualifications, warning against emotional overreactions toward day care centers. Yet his work was still picked up by media outlets the country over, and by conservative commentators hell-bent on using it to prove that the only appropriate kind of parenting was the kind in which the mother stayed at home.

In *Backlash*, Susan Faludi chronicled the mass panic evident in news headlines such as, "Mommy Don't Leave Me Here!," "Day Care Can Be Dangerous to Your Child's Health," and "When Child Care Becomes Child Molesting." This nationwide confusion and media-led hysteria around non-maternal child care eventually led to scores of day care center workers being accused of horrific kinds of child abuse—from sexual abuse to satanic rituals.

One of the more high-profile cases was the McMartin Preschool in Manhattan Beach, California. In 1984, Ray Buckey; his sister Peggy Ann; mother, Peggy; and grandmother, Virginia McMartin, along with three other teachers, were arrested for sexually abusing children after Buckey was accused of assaulting a two-year-old boy. Buckey was originally released because of a lack of evidence, but after police wrote letters to notify parents at the school, children started to come forward after being questioned (in leading ways) by their parents and therapists. They described satanic rituals, mutilated animals, and underground tunnels beneath the school. No evidence was found for any of this. The 1987 trial of Buckey and his mother would be the longest and most expensive criminal trial in American history. Peggy was acquitted and the charges were eventually dropped against Buckey, but not before they had spent years in jail. (Videotapes of interviews with the children making the allegations showed that the interviewers were so suggestive as to be leading, and the McMartin trial along with other similar cases are now known as part of a national moral panic that occurred around the idea of day cares and abuse.)

In a 2001 article for *The New York Times,* Margaret Talbot wrote:[6]

> Our willingness to believe in ritual abuse was grounded in anxiety about putting children in day care at a time when mothers were entering the work force in unprecedented numbers. It was as though there were some dark, self-defeating relief in trading niggling everyday doubts about our children's care for our absolute worst fears—for a story with monsters, not just human beings who didn't always treat our kids exactly as we would like; for a fate so horrific and bizarre that no parent, no matter how vigilant, could have ever prevented it.

Today, our panic over day care has turned into something else. Instead of an overwhelming fear that we're doing the wrong thing, we've channeled our anxiety into over-the-top justifications that we're doing the absolute right thing. Middle- and upper-class mothers battle it out on Urban-Baby.com over whether stay-at-home moms are doing better by their kids than working moms or if nannies are far superior to child care. They've gone from worrying about satanic day care workers to lobbying friends to help their children get into exclusive preschools. But the guilt remains—as does the gendered expectation that this is something only mothers should worry about. And while the mainstream media has become a bit better (though not substantially so) at parsing out moral panic and fear-based studies warning parents against outside care for their children, there are still plenty of people who seem to exist to stoke the fires of parental controversy and make women question their work/life decisions.

DO IT FOR YOURSELF

In Caitlin Flanagan's 2006 book, *To Hell with All That: Loving and Loathing Our Inner Housewife,* the controversial author argued that women who worked outside the home and weren't "at-home moms" were missing out on the joys of parenthood. She writes:

> The kind of relationship formed between a child and a mother who is home all day caring for him is substantively different from that formed between a child and a woman who is gone many hours a week. The former relationship is more intimate, more private, more filled with moments of maternal frustra-

tion—and even despair—and with more moments of the transcendence that comes only from mothering a small child.

When Flanagan isn't implicitly suggesting that stay-at-home parenting is best, she's explicitly knocking you out with the concept. In a 2004 article for *The Atlantic,* "How Serfdom Saved the Women's Movement," Flanagan[7] tells her readers that if they have a nanny, they better be prepared to lose the love of their children.

> To con oneself into thinking that the person who provides daily physical care to a child is not the one he is going to love in a singular and primal way—a way obviously designed by nature herself to cleave child to mother and vice versa—is to ignore one of the most fundamental truths of childhood. Just as women, often despite their fervent desires to the contrary, tend to fall in love with the men they sleep with, so do small children develop an immediate and consuming passion for the person who feeds and rocks and bathes them every day. It's in the nature of the way they experience love.

Flanagan managed—and still does—to tap into the parental anxiety so many women feel and to twist the knife. Perhaps the reason she's so adept at hitting a nerve, is that her own anxiety and ambivalence—and often times hypocrisy—are simmering just beneath the surface.

In an *Elle* magazine profile[8] of the writer, interviewer Laurie Abraham describes Flanagan as a bundle of contradictions: She complains about extravagant birthday parties for children, but has big soirees for her own; she warns of nannies stealing your children's love from you, but employs one herself. "I don't begrudge Flanagan her luxuries, but she's so oppressed by them," Abraham wrote.

It has also not been lost on Flanagan's numerous and vo-
ciferous critics, however, that the author—despite position-
ing herself as an "at-home" mother—had a full-time nanny,
housekeepers, even a "personal organizer" that worked for her.
Critics imagined that moments of "transcendence" were probably a lot easier to come by when you had a fulfilling career as
a well-known writer and employees to help you with the minutiae of parenting.

Joan Walsh at Salon.com wrote in a scathing review, "Everyone knows Caitlin Flanagan isn't a stay-at-home mother,
she's an accomplished writer who plays a stay-at-home mom
in magazines and on TV. . . . [S]he had a full-time nanny
when her twin sons were infants and she was trying to be a
novelist; then she wrote about modern womanhood and
family life for the *Atlantic Monthly* after they hit preschool;
now, with her boys in grade school, she's got a great gig at the
New Yorker. So how is she not a career woman who's also a
mom?"

Of course, Flanagan is hardly the first "professional stay-
at-home mom." Anti-feminist writer and activist Phyllis
Schlafly, who has six children, has been on the speaking and
media circuit for decades arguing that women's place is in the
home and with their children. (Unless you're her, it seems.)
And in a riveting 2006 *New York Times* column,[9] Terry Martin Hekker told the story of writing an op-ed for the paper in
1981 extolling the virtues of being a housewife, which turned
into a book and speaking career, only to get dumped on her
fortieth wedding anniversary. "I, however briefly, became the
authority on homemaking as a viable choice for women . . .
I lectured on the rewards of homemaking and housewifery.
[I] spoke to rapt audiences about the importance of being
there for your children as they grew up, of the satisfactions of

'making a home,' preparing family meals and supporting your hard-working husband."

After Hekker's husband divorced her, she wrote, "he got to take his girlfriend to Cancun, while I got to sell my engagement ring to pay the roofer." When Hekker filed her first non-joint tax return, she realized that she had become eligible for food stamps.

Hekker's story gets to an all-important point in the child care debate that needs revisiting—perhaps professional care for children isn't just good for children's well-being, it's integral for women's self-sufficiency. We can't take care of our children very well if at some point in our lives we won't even have the skills to take care of ourselves.

Hekker says, "For a divorced mother, the harsh reality is that the work for which you do get paid is the only work that will keep you afloat." It's a reality check in a conversation that's so often mired in middle-class and upper-middle-class privilege.

CAN MEN HAVE IT ALL?

For the first time in American history, men want to spend more time with their families and less time at work. Dads are desperate for more flexible solutions to *their* work/life balance—but what happens when they get it?

According to a 2011 report from the Families and Work Institute,[10] men are experiencing more work/life conflicts than ever before. Over the last thirty years, women's level of conflict over career and parenting hasn't changed significantly, but men's has substantially risen. In 1977, 34 percent of men reported work/life conflict—in 2008 that number jumped to

49 percent. Married fathers with jobs whose wives also have jobs were more likely to report dissatisfaction with their work/ life balance; 60 percent reported feeling conflict. In 1977 only 35 percent did.

The study also reported that men "are taking more overall responsibility for the care of their children," according to their partners. (In this case, "taking responsibility" meant taking care of the children themselves and managing other child care arrangements.)

Among the couples surveyed in 2008, men who said their female partners take the most responsibility for children were no longer in the majority—58 percent thought as much in 1992, but only 46 percent did in 2008. Similarly, 49 percent of men said they take on an equal amount of child care—up from 41 percent in 1992. Now, what men think they do and what wives think their husbands do has historically been pretty disparate. But in this report, the women surveyed agreed that their partners were taking more responsibility for children. In 1992, 73 percent of women said they took on the bulk of child care, in 2008 that number dropped to 66 percent. Also in 2008, 30 percent of women said that their spouse shared child care duties, up from 21 percent in 1992.

Men have also increased the amount of time that they spend with their children from two to three hours. Working mothers' time with children has remained the same at about 3.8 hours a day.

Another 2011 report, "The New Dad: Caring, Committed and Conflicted,"[11] from Boston College, surveyed almost one thousand fathers with full-time jobs at four different Fortune 500 companies about work/life conflict and balance issues. The report found that 77 percent of fathers want to spend more time with their kids, and that most identified their home life as a huge part of their identity; two thirds agreed with the statement, "To me, my work is only a small part of who I am." The researchers also found that more than 75 percent of the fathers reported using flextime informally or formally, that more than half worked from home at least some of the time, and 27 percent used compressed workweeks. The fathers that did take advantage of flextime were more likely to like their jobs than those who didn't.

There's no doubt that fathers' roles have changed significantly over the last few decades. They're more likely to spend more time with their kids, to expect more equitable (but not yet equal) breakdowns of domestic labor, and to seek out more flexible and family-friendly work policies. However, there are still significant hurdles — particularly in terms of gendered attitudes around what constitutes care, "family time," and time off.

When Steven Rhoads[12] of the University of Virginia, and his son, Christopher Rhoads, looked at almost two hundred married, tenure-track professors with children under two years old, they found something interesting about the way that parental leave was used.

Sixty-nine percent of the women they surveyed took maternity leave after birth, but only 12 percent of the men did (even though, in their cases, it was paid). That's not particularly unusual — there's still a lot of stigma around men taking time off for parental duties, so many men don't do it or don't fight for paternity leave. But here's an interesting bit: Those men who *did* take parental leave were found to perform substantially less child care duties than their partners. In fact, the report showed that male professors were using the time off to conduct research and publish papers, an act, the researchers say, that "puts their female colleagues at a disadvantage." One female in the report said, "If women and men are both granted parental leaves and women recover/nurse/do primary care and men do some care and finish articles, there's a problem."

Rhoads also noted, "Most of the academics in our study said they believe that husbands and wives should share equally, but almost none did so." So while changed attitudes are a step in the right direction, there needs to be a more fundamental, and tangible, shift of actual day-to-day care.

Similarly, while there has been a lot of media attention given to stay-at-home fathers ("The Rise of the Stay-at-Home Dad!"), they still remain statistical anomalies. There are only 165,000 fathers in the United States who provide stay-at-home care for their children, compared to 5.6 million women who do so.

What's more frequent than stay-at-home dads—but much less reported on—is single fathers. In 2010 there were 1.8 million single fathers in the United States—about 15 percent of single parents. Nine percent of those fathers were raising three or more children, while holding a full-time job. But working fathers doing double duty during the day and at home aren't as interesting as their stay-at-home counterparts.

The truth about fathers, sadly, is still largely unknown because of the way their roles are denigrated, not just culturally but politically as well—their care work is categorized as "baby sitting" by the Census Bureau, and workplace policies frequently exclude men from parental leave. When men have opportunities to take on more care-giving roles, they often shun them—so it's necessary to ensure that the cultural stigma against equal and involved fatherhood ends and that men are taught early on that they're just as capable as women to be caretakers.

The Boston College researchers recommended that men be given more time—through paternity leave that is substantial and used for caretaking—to develop their parenting skills. When men are left out of early infant and child care, they're more likely to feel as if they're not cut out for the duties. It's time to implement policies that will support a change in attitudes around gender and child care.

THE TRUTH ABOUT CHILD CARE

For most American women, the argument over whether to be an at-home mother or an at-work mother is a pointless one—it's a fight over a "choice" that few women have. Most American parents work because they have to—the privilege of a few of *not* needing an income cannot be overstated. It's no surprise then that most children with working mothers are cared for by someone else. According to the Census Bureau,[13] 24 percent of children from infants to three years old are in center-based child care, while 19.4 percent are cared for by grandparents, and 18.6 percent are cared for by their fathers. By the time children are toddlers, from three to six years old, about half of them will be in some sort of center-based care.

The costs for this care vary, but statistics show that the poorer a family is, the more money it is likely to pay for child care. The Department of Health and Human Services recommends that parents don't spend more than 10 percent of their income on child care. But according to the Census Bureau, in families with working mothers and incomes below the poverty line, child care takes up a third of household costs.

For some mothers, it's actually become more financially sound to take their children out of child care, quit work, and go on public assistance than to keep their kids in day care. *The New York Times* reported in May 2010[14] that because of cuts to state-subsidized child care centers, some mothers are choosing welfare over trying to make ends meet with high care costs.

And a 2010 study by the National Association of Child Care Resource and Referral Agencies[15] found that the cost of center-based care in forty states is actually more expensive than college tuition. This was particularly true for child care for infants—in Washington, D.C., New York, and Wyoming the costs for having a baby in day care were actually more than double the costs for a year's tuition at a public university. The organization also reported that over the last decade the cost of child care in this country has increased twice as fast as the median family income. For some families, the monthly costs for child care exceeded that of rent or mortgage.

The consequence of believing that mothers, and only mothers, should take care of their kids—that it's our duty for the good of children and society—is that we don't have a national child care system that works. Why bother if moms are the natural caretaker? Yet for all of our rhetoric about respecting mothers and parenthood, the United States is the only industrialized nation without paid maternity leave, putting families and children at severe economic risk. And due to the distinctly American belief that child care is a personal—not a political—issue, there is very little political or social momentum behind changing the status quo.

Historian and journalist Ruth Rosen, writing in *The Nation,* has said that the media and culture consistently reinforce that the "care crisis" in America is an individual problem, not a societal one.[16] "Books, magazines and newspapers offer American women an endless stream of advice about how to maintain their 'balancing act,' how to be better organized and more efficient or how to meditate, exercise and pamper themselves to relieve their mounting stress. Missing is the very pragmatic proposal that American society needs new policies that will restructure the workplace and reorganize family life."

Supporting structural, rather than personal, change is one missing piece of the work/life balance puzzle—the other is battling the mother-as-sole-care-provider ideal. Until we take that on, until women are no longer thought of as the default caretaker, there won't be enough cultural support to implement systemic changes that help parents.

And once parents don't see themselves as the sole provider of physical and emotional support for their children—once the idea of total motherhood has been put to rest—the guilt, shame, and unhappiness that comes along with being unable to be everything to your kids at all times will slowly die out.

FIVE

"The Hardest Job in the World"

> To call this a "job" is a dangerous simplification. In doing so, we run the risk of viewing our children, their environments and their lives as our "projects." Our goals. And of feeling that we must develop them, shape them and deliver them to the world as a product we naturally want to polish and perfect. But they're not, and in the end, there's painfully little about them that we truly determine.
>
> — *Sharon Bialy, blogger, Veronica's Nap*

THERE'S NO DOUBT that parenting—mothering espe-cially—is hard work. There's a certain look that moms get that's difficult to describe . . . all I know is that in the same way I can spot a heroin addict on the street, I can spot a mom. Caring for children leaves you haggard. (Believe me, I know—the under-eye circles I used to get after too many cocktails are now permanent fixtures on my face.) So I will not argue when someone says that mothering is hard.

But let's be honest—it's not the hardest. And as much as I love my daughter, I don't believe caring for her is the *most* important thing I'll ever do either. Yet in my relatively short time as a parent, I've heard from dozens of people telling me that what I'm doing is the hardest, most important job in the world. I'm not alone; we've all heard this sentiment a hundred times over. Even "Tiger Mom" Amy Chau says parenting was the hardest thing she's ever done.

Do American moms really believe that diaper changing trumps pediatric oncology? Or that child rearing is harder than being a firefighter or a factory worker?

And if we do believe the hype, if full-time motherhood really is the hardest job in the world, why isn't it paid? If it's the most rewarding, then why do so many of us have other people care for our children? And if parenting is the most important job in the world, why on earth aren't more men lining up to quit their frivolous-by-comparison day jobs in order to work for the world's most important (and littlest) employers?

Now, this idea—that parenting is the most difficult job in the world—may just be cultural hyperbole, but it's also a lie that too many of us have bought into. As one mom on the popular parenting website Babble commented,

> Whenever my guy friends try to tell me that my "job" ain't so bad I ask them what other job is 24/7, no sick days, no breaks, requires infinite patience, complete self-sacrifice, the acceptance of abuse, complete responsibility for every minute of every day in the life of another, and has no option to quit. Motherhood is tough because we have no idea what we're getting into until the day we're locked in for life to a job we must believe is the most rewarding in life.

The last sentence is where the truth comes home to roost: We *must* believe that parenting is the most rewarding, the hardest, and the most important thing we will ever do. Because if we don't believe it, then the diaper changing, the mind-numbing *Dora* watching, the puke cleaning, and the "complete self-sacrifice" that we're "locked in for life to" is all for nothing. We must believe it because the truth is just too damn depressing.

A MOTHER'S WORK IS NEVER DONE

In her best-selling book, *The Price of Motherhood: Why the Most Important Job in the World Is Still the Least Valued,* Ann Crittenden argued that there was a disconnect between the way motherhood is revered and the way it's tangibly valued culturally and economically. "All of the lip service to motherhood still floats in the air, as insubstantial as clouds of angel dust," she wrote. We say motherhood is important, but we sure don't act that way.

Crittenden believes that if Americans were going to talk the talk, we should walk the walk. Her solution is for society to start valuing motherhood with "across-the-board recognition—in the workplace, in the family, in the law, and in social policy—that someone has to do the necessary work of raising children and sustaining families." I agree. But Crittenden's argument stems from the idea that motherhood is just as important as the empty platitudes and Mother's Day cards would have us believe. To be sure, we need to make life easier (and fairer) for moms by valuing their work domestically, socially, and politically. But we also need a fundamental shift in the way we over-value mothering in women. Because if women continue to believe that the most important thing they can do is raise children—and that their children need to be the center of their universe—then the longer that American women will go unrecognized and undermined in public life, and the more frantic and perfectionist we'll become in our private and parental lives.

After all, there's something telling in the way that so many mothers are desperate to believe that their parenting is the most perfect, invaluable resource in their child's life. The mere suggestion that motherhood isn't the most important job in the world is likely to be met with the wrath of overworked moms everywhere.

Meagan Francis is a married mother of five, four boys and one girl, who lives in Michigan. In addition to caring for her family, Francis is the author of two books on motherhood, and a speaker and a blogger who writes about being the parent of a large brood. If anyone could lay claim to having a difficult job, she could. Yet in a 2009 essay,[1] Francis argued against the common claim that mothering is "the hardest job in the world."

> Personally, I prefer not to think of mothering my kids as a job, so much as a relationship—not to undermine what it is I do all day, most days, for thousands of days so far and thousands of days to come; but to give myself a break. If motherhood is my job, then I've got somebody to answer to, expectations to meet, performance reviews to face. And when my kids move out of the house or move on to a less dependent stage in life, I don't want to feel like I've just been pink-slipped.
>
> [I]f the work of being a mom is really as difficult as being a migrant farm worker or the leader of a nation, then maybe we're doing it wrong. Maybe the bar has been set too high. Or maybe we're all trying a little too hard.

After all, she writes, taking care of kids is not exactly digging ditches—even if you do have five of them. Francis was swiftly attacked by the parenting community in an online firestorm. One blogger wrote[2] that as soon as she finished reading, she "wanted to reach through the computer screen and throttle" Francis. Another commented, "I have worked the fields of organic farms, cared for multiple screaming children during the day, and working impossibly long hours at an office with a hateful and demanding boss. You know what? Motherhood has been more difficult than all of these experiences put together. Who are you to tell me that I am a wimp or that coal miners have a more difficult job?"

A male commenter even suggested that the future of children everywhere was at stake if women failed to take this most "important" job seriously enough: "If mothers do not treat the raising of their children as a world-changing career, then that job will inevitably be left to TV, movies, songs, school & the government, and we all see where that has gotten us today around the world."

To other moms, Francis was criticizing their very moral centers. One mother wrote that even though she preferred to do "work-work," she grins and bears it—motherhood—because she believes it's the "right thing to do."

> I woke up this morning and my job so far has consisted of playing blocks, making breakfast, trying to straighten the kitchen while being asked to play blocks more . . . being ordered to do puzzles while I am trying to finish making breakfast . . . somewhere in there, I had to clean two potty poops within five minutes, do the ceremonial sticker chart and treats, read a story . . . However, I know its the right thing to do, since we don't need the money, to stay home and nurture my guy. [That's] one reason I get so annoyed with people who choose to plop their kids with someone else when they don't need the money. Do your time, ladies!

Do your time. Locked in for life. When motherhood keeps getting likened to a prison sentence, you know something is very wrong. Which it's no surprise that other mommy bloggers responded to the controversy with relief. Sasha Brown-Worsham, a Boston-based mom writing at My Wombinations wrote[3] that she saw Francis's essay as a "call to moms to stop the madness and stop killing ourselves to make sure our children are properly stimulated, full of organic foods/breastmilk and happy at all times." She added,

> This is where the misery comes in. Because I have been crazy in many ways with my kids. In addition to the constant guilt, I am always worried that Sam is not getting enough stimulation. On the odd chance we spend a day at home, I feel horribly guilty. I derive little joy from motherhood at times because I am always worried about what is next or whether Sam had enough intellectual stimulation that day. I try very hard to balance the play—the trips to the park, the long walks, the Children's/science museum/aquarium—with the intellectual—the helping her with her reading, art class, Spanish class, ballet/gymnastics. It can be exhausting, though, that constant worry that I did not do enough, feed her brain enough, let her blow off steam enough. It is the constant worry that DOES make motherhood so stressful.

Even the mother who admitted to wanting to throttle Francis—thirty-four-year-old Kristi Gaylord—admitted that part of what set her off about the essay was the pressure she puts on herself. "Perhaps we're all trying way too hard to be 'perfect mothers' and in killing ourselves to achieve this impossible standard, motherhood becomes less of a relationship and more of a job."

I will readily admit to trying too hard and putting too much pressure on myself. I constantly feel inadequate. I always feel as if I'm failing. And I never feel at the end of the day that yes, each of my children had enough of my time and enough social, developmental, and cultural enrichment. When I look at things this way, then yes. Motherhood is a job, and one at which I am not particularly succeeding.

It's this—the guilt, the self-flagellation, the pursuit of a perfection that doesn't exist—that is sucking the joy out of motherhood. It's also why the notion of parenting as the "hardest job in the world" isn't just cold comfort we give ourselves while attending to the minutiae of mothering, but an oppressive standard making us feel worthless. After all, when Oprah dedicated a 2009 episode of her eponymous show to mothers (which she claimed would be a "judgment-free zone, a sisterhood of motherhood where anything goes"), she declared, "moms have the toughest job in the world if you're doing it right." Yikes.

I'm sure that Oprah meant this in the kindest way possible—that mothers have an incredibly tough job, that they're overworked and underappreciated. But the sentiment that women overwhelmingly hear is that if we don't think parenting is the most difficult thing we've ever done, if we don't find it exhausting and draining and killing our sex lives . . . well, we're doing it wrong. Do your time, ladies.

And boy are we ever doing it. Parenting requires cleaning and cooking and feeding and chauffeuring and teaching and thousands of other necessary things that make up a child's day. This daily caretaking is even more complicated for full-time moms and mothers who want their child's day not just to be good, but amazing—moms who believe every hour of their child's life should be enriching and filled with intellectual stimulation. Because good mothering is no longer just about raising well-adjusted kids. It's about raising the smartest, coolest, artiest, most organic-eating, most well-behaved, and fastest video-game-weaned kids of all time. Whether you call them helicopter parents or CEO moms—there's no doubt that "over-parenting" is everywhere and mothers are leading the way. They're making their own organic baby food while scheduling piano lessons, ballet class, and French tutors. They're spending all day online discussing the right kind of baby wrap and whether their DS or DD (dear son or dear daughter) is reading enough, rolling over soon enough, or could be getting any number of colds, flus, or viruses that are going around their neighborhood.

We mock these moms as neurotic overachievers who are obsessed with their kids, but perhaps their zealous parenting is just the understandable outcome of expecting smart, driven women to find satisfaction in spit-up. All of the energy that they could be—and maybe should be—spending in the public sphere is directed at their children because they have no other place to put it. And because, like Kristi, so many feel like they're failing, I find it difficult to accept that this is simply the way women are happiest.

Though not all mothers fall for the trap of believing that parenting is the most important job they'll ever have (or that it must be the hardest for the good of their children), it's still a dangerous idea that moves beyond greeting cards and daytime talk shows. Telling women—because this is not a "compliment" levied at dads—that motherhood is the most valuable job in the world is not just a patronizing pat on the head. As Crittenden noted, it's a way to placate overworked moms without giving them the social and political support they actually need to make their lives better.

The cultural insistence that motherhood is the most "important" job in the world is a smart way to satiate unappreciated women without doing a damn thing for them. It's an empty cliché that strategically keeps women in the home through the sly insistence that motherhood is much more valuable than any job that women could have in the public sphere. Why become a high-paid lawyer or an influential politician when motherhood awaits? In fact, using motherhood as a way to keep women out of the public sphere has a long history in this country.

Today, the message may be different but the outcome is the same. Women are made to feel that if they don't fulfill their natural role (and smile while doing it!), they're doing a great disservice to their children, their country, and even to themselves. Dr. Laura Schlessinger, a popular conservative radio personality, frequently calls motherhood the most important job in the world. In her book *In Praise of Stay-at-Home Moms,* Schlessinger—who has a PhD in physiology—argues that the joys of parenthood far outweigh any satisfaction women could take out of working in the public sphere. The book praises these women as those "who know in their hearts that staying home to raise their children is the right choice for the whole family."

Of course, it is also possible for a child brought up mostly in day care, or by nannies and/or babysitters, to be successful, personally and professionally. I wouldn't dream of suggesting that there are any real benefits to children from having at-home parents; it's just a choice, like French or vinaigrette dressing on your salad. Isn't it? Well, sure that's right, because if you knew you were going to be recycled and come back as an infant with a choice, you'd choose a mommy, a nanny, a babysitter, or a day-care worker for yourself with equal enthusiasm—right?

Ah guilt, few do it better than Dr. Laura. When an interviewer with the *Wall Street Journal* asked Schlessinger about the families in which mothers staying at home were not financially feasible, she replied, "If we truly believe in something and cherish it, we find a way to make it happen."[4] Fairy dust, perhaps? Guilt and unrealistic financial planning aside, the real message Schlessinger is selling is that women are made to be mothers. "My heart just hurts [for working women]—because when you get those pudgy arms around your neck, and being told you're someone's lullaby—the fact that a woman would miss that is so, so sad." Never mind that working mommies get hugs, too, but when you try to make women believe that the most important thing they'll ever do is become mothers, "experts" often have to fall back on guilt because there is little else holding women in the home.

Take Sasha, a mother and commenter at Babble:

I have my 2.5-year-old daughter enrolled in Spanish class, gymnastics, art class, preschool and ballet and I have to schlep her to all of these activities, fight with her about it all and still manage to get in the basics of reading to her, nursing her little brother, cuddling her, feeding her healthy/nutritious meals and time at the park. But the alternative makes me feel so guilty, it is not even worth considering. Is it a "job"? Well, maybe not. But it is certainly the hardest thing I have ever done in my life—I also think it really depends on your definition of "hard." Is it harder to have your head in someone else's poop, scrubbing the toilets or harder to feel almost constant guilt and emotionally drained every day? In parenthood, you get both.

It's not just the guilt that's dangerous—because when you're telling women that their natural role is only that of a mother, it's that much easier to convince them that they don't need to be doctors, scientists, and politicians.

And, of course, if parenting is so rewarding and so important, why aren't more men staying home to do it? After all, men like important jobs, don't they?! But this is just an easy excuse—framed as the ultimate compliment—for men who want women to continue to do the lion's share of child rearing. David Brooks, in a 2006 *New York Times* op-ed titled "The Year of Domesticity,"[5] for example, argued that the domestic sphere is "the realm of unmatched influence." He goes on to say, "If there is one thing we have learned over the past generation, it is that a child's I.Q., mental habits and destiny are largely shaped in the first few years of life, before school or the outside world has much influence."

Now, of course it's easy for someone like Brooks to write that "power is in the kitchen," when he's working from a cozy columnist's desk. As Salon writer Rebecca Traister snarked in response, "if [Brooks is] really so aggrieved by his lack of power as an IQ-builder for the next generation, perhaps he should surrender his post to work full-time at a child-care facility."[6] Something tells me he won't be abandoning his job anytime soon. And really, how insulting is it to suggest that the best thing women can do is raise other people to do incredible things? I'm betting some of those women would like to do great things of their own.

A similar argument popped up in a "progressive" book group that my husband was a part of several years ago. One week, instead of a book, the group—made up mostly of men in their twenties—read an article by Ruth Rosen in *The Nation* called the "Care Crisis." The article laid out why caretaking done by women—whether it was mothering or caring for elderly parents—had been relegated to something Americans thought of as private decisions rather than the political issues they were. The men vociferously agreed—our nation needed subsidized child care, more flextime, and paid family leave! These sexist policies needed to be changed! But when Andrew asked how many of them would be willing to marry someone who expected equally shared parenting and domestic responsibilities, you could hear crickets.

Over the course of the conversation, most of the men grudgingly admitted to wanting a partner who would stay at home with any children they may have—an option that the men would never consider for themselves. Most also figured that the women in their lives would be more than happy to take on the primary role of caregiver because that's what they were best suited for. (Never mind that these men were dating editors, writers, and activists at the time.) These are progressive, pro same-sex marriage, anti-racism dudes who are all about changing policy—just not their lives.

This disconnect between the personal and the political remains, and today—forty years after Betty Friedan tried to free women from domestic drudgery—women are still stuck believing that the most important thing they can do for their children is be there for them. All. The. Time.

Now, do I believe that my labor as a mother is important and valuable? Absolutely. (In fact, I think parenthood should be a paid venture.) I simply don't think that putting every bit of energy I have into parenting—at the expense of my career, marriage, and social life—will be the difference between Layla becoming homeless or the president. But too many women are made to believe that every tiny decision they make—from pacifiers to flash cards—will have a lasting impact on their child. It's a recipe for madness. It also reveals an overblown sense of self-importance. Before you throw this book across the room or frantically Google me for an email address to send hate mail to, hear me out.

We believe that in the same way we're making our children the center of our lives (and, wow, I can't wait to see the entitled kids that come out of that parenting philosophy!), we are the center of our children's lives. That they need their mothers above all else, despite evidence to the contrary. Vast amounts of research show that children do best when they're raised by a community of people—parents, grandparents, friends, and neighbors. It's in our DNA—we are social beings, and we should be raised as such. Yes, mothers are important, but not because we are women or because we're biologically related (or not) to our children. We're important because we're one of the people that love and care for a growing human. But if we want to take some joy in that experience, we need to let go of the notion that we are the only ones who can do it correctly, and that if we are doing it right, it should mean some sort of suffering or tremendous self-sacrifice.

This isn't to say that women shouldn't care about parenting or make their public and work lives adjust to their parenting lives. I'm also not arguing that women shouldn't stay home with their children (well, not yet anyway). When I had Layla, Andrew and I were deliberate about our work/family decisions. We decided to start trying for pregnancy when both of us would be working from home, to ensure that we had the most equitable breakdown of child care possible. (Of course, working from home would later be the privilege and blessing that would get us through Layla's early birth and long hospital stay.) I think it's smart to plan how parenting will fit into our lives; I simply don't think that it needs to be the centerpiece of who we are and what we do.

When Layla was born early and required special care after her long hospital stay, I, unfortunately, didn't have a choice in deciding whether or not she would be the center of my life. She just was; her health and survival depended on it. But it's not something I cherished, and instead I longed for Layla's independence (and my freedom). I don't want to be the center of her universe, and as much as I love Layla, I don't want her to be the center of mine. I'm a mother, but I'm other things, too, and my other desires, ambitions, and beliefs are as much a part of me, maybe even more, than being a parent.

The truth is, we can simultaneously love parenting, find it fulfilling and valuable, while also recognizing that the minutiae of our mothering isn't as critical as society would have us believe. We can love our children without believing the world revolves around them. We can derive pleasure from caretaking without thinking it's the most important thing we'll ever do or the biggest contribution we'll make to society. And we can be exhausted, overworked moms while still recognizing that there are plenty of other jobs that are harder, and yes, even more important. Because when we see parenting for what it is—a relationship, not a job—we can free ourselves from the expectations and the stifling standards that motherhood-as-employment demands.

So yes, let's make sure that parenting is valued, but let's value it a little bit less when it comes to women.

SIX

Mother Knows Best

Follow your instincts. That's where
true wisdom manifests itself.
— *Oprah Winfrey*

T HESE DAYS, EVERYONE is an expert. Thanks largely to
the Internet, anyone who publishes a blog, has a Twitter
following of more than a thousand people, or a Tumblr
site that gets occasionally reblogged is considered an authority in something or other. For women, who are publishing
mothering blogs and populating online parenting forums at
lightning speed, this kind of recognition has been a long time
coming.

From the 1970s hand-mirror vaginal checks to birthing in
the bathtub with Ricki Lake, if modern feminism has taught
us anything it's that we're the bosses of our own bodies and
experts of our own lives. The personal is political, right?

But the downside of telling women that we know it all
is that we've *become* know-it-alls, holding ourselves to the
monumental expectation of being the ultimate authority in

all things parental — to our own and our children's detriment.
We're not just moms any more; thanks to the wealth of information online and the democratization of expertise, mothers now feel like they have to be teachers, nurses, nutrition-
ists, and even scientists. (If they're not actually these things
already!)

While there's something empowering and encouraging
about women taking control of their lives and shunning traditional knowledge, there's also something dangerous there.
It's not all joyous home births and La Leche League meetings,
after all. In fact, mothers' belief that their maternal instinct
trumps all has already sparked a nationwide health crisis — the
anti-vaccination movement.

The notion of maternal love is an old one, but maternal
"instinct" — the idea that women have a certain natural understanding or knowledge of what their children need — is newer.
It's a modern invention that came about in the Western world
as medicine and nutrition improved and infant mortality became less widespread; previously, infants were at such a high
risk for death that children often went unnamed until they
were a year or two years old.

Elisabeth Badinter argued in her 1981 book *Mother Love:
Myth and Reality* that the idea of maternal instinct is socially constructed, not a biological given. Badinter pointed to
mothers in eighteenth-century France; a time in which almost
all — about 95 percent — of newborns in areas like Paris were
sent to wet nurses. The practice led to high rates of infant
mortality — both because babies breastfed by wet nurses were
more likely to die and because wet nurses were more likely to
abandon their own children when they got employed suckling
someone else's. Badinter wrote that if maternal instinct were
indeed natural and "spontaneous," how could mothers sim-

ply send their children off, abandoning them? "I am not questioning maternal love," she wrote. "I am questioning maternal instinct."

MOTHERS' SHOT IN THE ARM

Elyse Anders, of Dallas, Texas, was pregnant with her second child when the swine flu scare hit the United States. Schools were shutting down, the president declared a national emergency, and the Centers for Disease Control activated its Emergency Operations Center. By March 2010, the CDC estimated that 59 millions Americans had contracted swine flu, 265,000 were hospitalized, and 12,000 died of the virus. Thankfully, there was a vaccine—but not everyone was lining up to get it.

"It was terrifying to see all of these people who were saying they weren't going to get vaccinated," Anders told me. (Pregnant women are particularly susceptible to the disease.)

"I mean, perfectly healthy people were dropping dead of the flu, and people were refusing to get the vaccine?!"

Anders says that's when she decided she needed to "step up" her efforts and become more active on the issue. "I was always passionate about science and critical thinking," she said. But it was being a mother that really put the anti-vaccination issue on her radar. The thirty-four-year-old mother started writing for the science and skepticism blog Skepchick,[1] and founded Hug Me I'm Vaccinated, an educational outreach campaign that encourages parents to vaccinate their children.

There has always been a small percentage of the population that refuses to vaccinate—but according to the Centers for Disease Control, that's to be expected. So long as about 95 percent of the population gets vaccinations, the majority of Americans will be safe. But what's been happening in recent years is that unvaccinated children (and adults) are now concentrated in small areas.

"It's usually upper-middle-class neighborhoods—which is not what you would expect," Anders says. "But you end up with these communities where you only have 20 to 50 percent of their kids being vaccinated. So you end up with clusters, and that's where we have outbreaks, and then those spread."

Indeed, that's just what happened in 2011 when the United States saw the largest measles outbreak in fifteen years—the CDC attributed it to small groups of unvaccinated children. In April 2011, an alternative private school in Floyd County, Virginia, had to shut down when half of its students got pertussis—also known as whooping cough. All of the students who contracted the virus were unvaccinated.

A resurgence of pertussis also cropped up in California in 2010 because of unvaccinated kids—it was the worst outbreak in over sixty years. Babies with pertussis will cough so often and so hard that the air is entirely forced out of their lungs and they inhale with a loud "whooping" noise. Ten infants died as a result of the outbreak in California. It is a horrible disease, a terrible way to die. So why would any parent put their child—and others' children—at risk by choosing not to vaccinate?

Seth Mnookin, author of *The Panic Virus: The True Story Behind the Vaccine-Autism Controversy,* says that today's parents simply don't have the type of personal experience with deadly infectious diseases that past generations had, but that there's also something specific about the way we raise children that makes parents now more skeptical of vaccines.

"To our generation of 'helicopter parents' there's something about following this blanket vaccination schedule that is just sensitive—it feels like someone is saying your child is not

special, we're not going to tailor this to your specific needs."
But of course, Mnookin jokes, likening vaccinations to something that need to be tailored to each specific child is like saying, "We're going to tailor oxygen intake to your child's specific needs, or bowel movements."

Mnookin tells me that even before his wife gave birth to
their first child, when a lot of their friends we're having kids,
he realized that "a lot of parents really felt that they were kind
of out to sea. Remarkably, because of how much money we
spend on books and manuals, when you go in that one second
from not being a parent to being a parent you discover what it
means to feel totally helpless."

In his book, Mnookin recalls a dinner party where a friend
couldn't quite explain why he was choosing not to vaccinate
his child—and why he had such distrust toward the medical community. Mnookin was intrigued. "It's an interesting
lens to examine this other sort of series of issues, which is
this sense of instinct—of 'knowing' something to be true and
making decisions based on that." Today, we call it maternal
instinct.

THE SICK SENSE

When Jenny McCarthy came on to the anti-vaccination/par-
enting scene, everything changed. The former *Playboy* bunny
turned nineties MTV personality turned anti-vaccination su-
perstar has used the idea of women's intuition to completely
change the landscape of the way parents think about caring
for their kids.

McCarthy caused a huge spike in the mainstreaming of
anti-vaccination thought after she started publicly writing
and talking about her son's autism—which she believed was

caused by the MMR vaccination. She's written eight books, appeared on *Oprah* to tell her story, and is now the president of Generation Rescue, an organization that claims to help parents "cure" their children of autism.

When McCarthy's son, Evan, was diagnosed with autism in 2005, McCarthy says that after the initial shock, she "got up, went to the computer and Googled the word 'autism.'" She claims that a year after putting Evan on a special diet, giving him particular vitamins, and changing his home environment, he was "un-diagnosed" as autistic. (Experts have since suggested that Evan never had autism, but in fact likely has Landau-Kleffner syndrome, a childhood neurological disorder that can have similar symptoms to autism.)

McCarthy's story is incredibly compelling and she's a perfect spokesperson for any cause: likable, beautiful, and comes with a built-in platform. While there's no doubt that McCarthy's star power lent credibility to this fringe movement, what really makes McCarthy so gripping to so many parents—especially mothers—is something much bigger. She's tapped into the one thing that so many American moms are looking for: validation. That their knowledge means something.

When McCarthy was confronted with a statement from the CDC during her 2007 *Oprah* appearance that pointed out the overwhelming scientific evidence against her, her response perfectly captured the sentiment of moms across the country: "My science is Evan. He's at home. That's my science."

So for a generation of parents—mothers especially—who are extremely uncomfortable with not feeling in control and increasingly more interested in trusting their own knowledge over experts, the anti-vaccination movement is perfect.

When a cause comes along that says: *You do the research, trust yourself, Big Pharma is trying to get one over on you,* that's a very seductive message to a population that is sick and tired of not being respected. That's why, in part, women tend to be more anti-vaccination than men. They're more vocal not only because they tend to be the ones that are making decisions about children, but they're also the ones who are more invested in the idea of their own knowledge as expertise.

"They do their research—and it's not that they're stupid, they find this information on alternative medical sites. The joke, and it was coined by McCarthy, is that they go to the University of Google," says Anders.

One problem with researching autism or vaccines on the Internet is that without a specific kind of expertise or context, it's easy to get caught up in false information. Anders points out that when you type "vaccine" into Google, the first hits aren't science based. "They're anti-vaccine sites that skew the data and terrify people," she says. "They'll instruct readers to go to the CDC site and tell you to look at the ingredients of a vaccine—and people see things like mercury and aluminum. If you're not science literate or understand why these things are important, that can be very scary."

And what many parents don't realize is the way in which Internet searches are biased. Google, for example, learns what you're interested in and will give you search results according to those interests. So let's say you search for "vaccine autism" and you click on a website that claims to show a connection between the disorder and vaccinations, the next time you do a similar search, Google will remember what you clicked on and show you like-minded results in your follow-up searches.

"Because the Internet is self referential, once you go down one trap door, it becomes increasingly hard to pull yourself out," Mnookin says. He also posits that because there's much less availability with medical professionals than in years past, parents are increasingly more likely to seek out information online. "If my parents had questions for my pediatrician there wasn't this sense that if they didn't get their questions answered in a fifteen-minute wellness visit that they were going to have to get another appointment and possibly pay out of pocket. . . . In this way, the medical community has really failed parents."

The medical establishment also failed women, specifically—which is why so many of them seek out information elsewhere. They have very good reasons to be skeptical of the medical establishment, particularly as it pertains to becoming a parent.

MEDICINE WOMEN

As indicated by the increase in maternal mortality in 2010, right now it's more dangerous for women to give birth in California than in Kuwait or Bosnia. Amnesty International reports that women in this country have a higher risk of dying due to pregnancy complications than women in forty-nine other countries (black women are almost four times as likely to die as white women). The United States spends more than any other country on maternal health care, yet our risk of dying or coming close to death during pregnancy or in childbirth remains unreasonably high. (During 2004 and 2005, more than sixty-eight thousand women almost died in childbirth.)

Women's health advocates say this disconnect is in part because of the way the health care system operates. Amnesty International, for example, points to discrimination and financial burdens that put women's and mother's health at risk. But others argue that in addition to systemic inequities, the medical community's obsession with pathologizing childbirth and trumping convenience over women's health is to blame.

Jennifer Block, author of *Pushed: The Painful Truth about Childbirth and Modern Maternity Care,* has documented how the rates of C-sections—a leading cause of complications and death in childbirth—sharply increase around lunchtime and at the end of the workday, when doctors want to grab something to eat or head home. The C-section rate in the United States is at an all-time high of 32 percent; that's almost one in three women giving birth via serious abdominal surgery. The rate is twice as high as recommended by the World Health Organization. Potential complications for C-sections are numerous, yet doctors are still performing the surgeries at increased rates.

The United States medical industry also has a long and terrifying history of forced sterilizations—particularly among the most marginalized groups of women. There was actually legislation in some states in the early 1900s that mandated the sterilization of mentally challenged and mentally ill women, as part of a national eugenics movement. In fact, in 1927, the Supreme Court ruled that sterilizing women did not violate the Constitution in *Buck v. Bell.* Justice Oliver Wendell Holmes wrote, "It is better for all the world, if instead of waiting to execute degenerate offspring for a crime, or let them starve for their imbecility, society can prevent those who are manifestly unfit from continuing their kind."

Women of color, Native American women, immigrant women, and low-income women were also targeted—often being sterilized without their knowledge or consent when they went to a hospital for another reason, such as giving birth. Under the Nixon administration, there was even Medicaid funding for such sterilizations. And in Puerto Rico, coercive practices by the government and medical community led to a whopping 35 percent sterilization rate among women there.

While legal sterilizations were still being performed up until the 1980s, even today certain women are pressured and coerced to use long-term birth control methods or be sterilized. Organizations like Project Prevention (previously named Children Requiring a Caring Kommunity, or CRACK) put up billboards in low-income neighborhoods offering women money to be sterilized.

And these are just two issues in a long history of American medicine mistreating and maligning women—from false diagnoses of hysteria in the eighteenth and nineteenth century to pharmacists today refusing to give women birth control because they don't like the idea of women having sex, there's no question that women have plenty of reasons to be distrustful. There's no doubt that America has historically ignored women's and mother's opinions, and moms are routinely told that they're being too neurotic and to trust the experts, even when that means going against their instincts. Thankfully, modern feminism has made it possible for women to regain control over their bodies—whether it's through access to birth control and abortion or by questioning the increasing medicalization of childbirth and the motives of doctors who infringe on women's reproductive freedoms.

But does a justifiable skepticism of the medical establishment mean that mothers should completely discount accepted medical and scientific knowledge in favor of their own supposed sixth sense?

The idea of maternal instincts simultaneously appeals to and appalls my feminist sensibilities. I trust women, it's what my politics and personal beliefs are largely based on. But the idea that women have some sort of female sixth sense is also right on par with the essentializing, somewhat naive contention that the world would be a better place if only women ran it. (Clearly the people who believe women are naturally more peaceful or maternal have never visited UrbanBaby.com.)

My skepticism of "maternal instincts" or "women's intuition" is also due largely to the fact that my own were so lacking. When I was sick with preeclampsia—my blood pressure dangerously high and just days away from my liver starting to fail—I was completely clueless. My "instincts" told me that my swollen face—a telltale sign of the disease—was because it was a hot summer and, hey, I was pregnant. I had gained a lot of weight that week (sudden weight gain is also a symptom) because, I thought, I had been on vacation and gorged on buttery lobster and days of desserts. The day before I was admitted to the hospital, I had lunch with my lovely editor for this very book, and despite my feet being so swollen that I considered cutting my ballet flats off in the cab ride home, I figured it was all par for the pregnancy course. It never occurred to me that I could be gravely ill. I needed a doctor to tell me that.

But I also understand why messages like Jenny McCarthy's—as dangerous as I think they are—resonate so deeply. When I was pregnant, nothing was more important to me than informing myself—it was my responsibility to educate myself and make the best decisions for my family and me. It's part and parcel of my feminism. And it made me feel powerful.

I was wary of books like *What to Expect When You're Expecting* and traditional ob-gyns. After all, I had watched Ricki Lake give birth in a bathtub in *The Business of Being Born* and had read Jennifer Block's wonderful book. I knew that the

medical establishment didn't necessarily have my best interest at heart. I knew that the rate of C-sections went up during lunch hours and right after six p.m. I knew that getting an
epidural during labor could lead to a domino effect in which
a C-section became much more likely. And I knew from my
own blogging and writing that pregnant women's rights are
routinely violated.

I was well aware that if I wanted to have the kind of prenatal care and delivery that I felt was best, I would have to fight
for it. After deciding that home birth wasn't for me (my husband and I were uncomfortable with how far away a drive the
nearest decent hospital was), I found an ob-gyn who preferred
"natural" birth; she also had midwives in her practice that
had privileges at St. Luke's-Roosevelt Birth Center. I ate organic food, exercised, and shunned the overzealous U.S. recommendations for pregnant women by having the occasional
glass of red wine.

Just two days before I was hospitalized—and less than a
week before my emergency C-section and Layla's birth—I
was leisurely touring St. Luke's-Roosevelt Birth Center, eyeing
the relaxation tubs. I was woefully underprepared for what
happened to me.

While Layla was in the NICU, the only sense of control
I had, the only "maternal" power, was my instincts and ability to trust myself. My husband and I gave ourselves a crash
course in premature infants—yes, using Google, among other
resources—but between trips back and forth to the hospital,
my own recovery, and the daily stress of having a sick child,
there was only so much we could learn. For the rest we had to
rely on experts.

Trusting people (strangers, really) with your child's health
is frightening. You put your child's life in someone's hands

MOTHER KNOWS BEST 89

and hope that they know what they're doing. The lack of control is core shaking. But sometimes you just don't have much of a choice—you have to let go.

The moments when we could exert control—when my knowledge and intuition made Layla safer—were incredibly comforting. One day when my mother went to visit Layla in the hospital, for example, she put her hands in the Isolette to hold Layla's hand and noticed that it was colder than usual. (The Isolette was constantly heated because Layla wasn't able to regulate her own body temperature yet.) It turns out that the heater had broken and the nurses hadn't noticed yet. Similarly, because I was the one who was with Layla the most often—NICU nurses are switched out often as a way to ensure they don't get too attached to any one baby—I tended to notice smaller issues before her doctors or nurses, like eye infections or when her breathing tubes were rubbing her nostrils raw.

These are all issues that I'm sure her caregivers would have figured out and remedied eventually, but being there and feeling like I could offer knowledge that would help my daughter gave me back a sense of control when I so often felt as if I had none. It was, for lack of a better non-overused word, empowering.

It's this sense of empowerment that has so many women turning away from traditional forms of expertise and tuning back into themselves—even if it means supporting dangerous health risks like non-vaccination.

And again, there's something feminist about letting women's voices—which have been historically ignored or maligned—come out in full force. We are all experts in terms of our own experiences, our lives. But the truth, as uncomfortable as it may make us, is that we don't know everything. It's tempting to think that we do, especially now when the expectation of motherhood (think Joan Wolf's "total motherhood") is that we have to know everything in order to be a good—or even just adequate—mother.

Here are just some of the things mothers are expected to know about their children: their exact weight, height, age in weeks, days, and hours; their last vaccination (no peeking at that record!); day care hours, day care pick-up, and day care rules about peanut butter or packing extra clothes; allergies and medical history; what foods they like and don't like (and at what temperature and consistency they like said foods); how many teeth they have, and if they've lost any teeth, how many; their favorite books, favorite toys, favorite colors, and favorite music; when their fingernails were last cut; the color of their feces, the shape and consistency of their everyday feces; if they've thrown up, how much, and if it was preceded by coughing; and so on and so on.

Here are some of the things we're expected to do: know how to deal with insurance companies; make appointments with the pediatrician, nutritionist, developmental specialist, and/or speech therapist; ensure there are enough diapers in the house, enough milk, enough wipes, enough pacifiers; remember to pay the babysitter, the nanny, or the day care; ask my mother to watch her (again?).

Yes, fathers do these things as well. But when dads know these intimate details of their child's life, they're considered heroes; when moms do, it's standard.

Living in the age of the expert mom means that maternal instinct isn't just about mom love anymore. It's a built-in expectation that truly loving and committed mothers are the absolute authority on everything having to do with their children—down to the very last dirty diaper.

The truth is, of course, that we're *not* experts in everything. Women aren't experts just by virtue of being women, or by being mothers. Doing research on Google does not put us on par with an inoculation researcher, and staying on top of the minutiae of our children's lives does not mean that we don't need help and support from actual experts.

It may be that American mothers are so desperate for power, recognition, and validation that we'd rather take on the burden of considering ourselves "expert" moms rather than change the circumstances that demand such an unreasonable role for us.

Believing that our maternal instinct somehow means we know more than anyone else not only puts undue pressure on ourselves and our ability to feel like good parents, but it also furthers the idea that there is such a thing as a natural, overwhelming mother love—a belief that actually falls apart when we take a closer look at the way children are really being treated.

But there's a difference between being well informed and empowered, and being burdened with thinking that you need to know *everything* in order to be a good parent.

TRUTH

SEVEN

Giving Up on Parenthood

I no longer wish to parent this child.

— *Part of a note pinned on a seven-year-old boy
who was placed alone on a plane to Russia*

Women's responses were assumed to be reflexive and
automatic, as inevitable as the uterine muscle contractions
that ushered her baby into the world. Such devotion
was subsumed under the scientific-sounding label
"maternal instinct." Accordingly, mothers who abandon
infants were viewed as unnatural. Even mothers who
merely feel ambivalent must need counseling.

— *Anthropologist Sarah Blaffer Hrdy*

N 2008, NEBRASKA DECRIMINALIZED child abandonment. The move was part of a "safe haven" law designed
to address increased rates of infanticide in the state. Like
other safe haven laws, parents in Nebraska who felt unpre-
pared to care for their babies could drop them off at a designated location without fear of arrest and prosecution. But

legislators made a major logistical error: They failed to implement an age limitation for dropped-off children.

Within just weeks of the law passing, parents started dropping off their kids. But here's the rub, none of them were infants. A couple of months in, thirty-six children had been left in state hospitals and police stations. Twenty-two of the children were over thirteen years old, and eight were between ten and twelve years old. A fifty-one-year-old grandmother dropped off a twelve-year-old boy. One father dropped off his entire family—nine children from ages one to seventeen. Others drove from neighboring states to drop off their children once they heard that they could abandon them without repercussion.

The Nebraska state government, realizing the tremendous mistake it had made, held a special session of the legislature to rewrite the law in order to add an age limitation. Governor Dave Heineman said the change would "put the focus back on the original intent of these laws, which is saving newborn babies and exempting a parent from prosecution for child abandonment. It should also prevent those outside the state from bringing their children to Nebraska in an attempt to secure services."[1]

On November 21, 2008, the last day that the safe haven law was in effect for children of all ages, a mother from Yolo County, California, drove over twelve hundred miles to the Kimball County Hospital in Nebraska where she left her fourteen-year-old son.

What happened in Nebraska begs the question: If there were no consequences, how many of us would give up our kids? After all, child abandonment is nothing new and it's certainly not rare in the United States. Over four hundred thousand children are in the foster care system waiting to be placed in homes, thousands of parents relinquish their children every year, and some are even sending their adoptive children back to their home countries with apology letters pinned like grocery lists to their chests. Whether it's because of hardship or not, many Americans are giving up on parenthood.

In February 2009, someone calling herself Ann logged onto the website Secret Confessions[2] and wrote three sentences: "I am depressed. I hate being a mom. I also hate being a stay at home mom too!" Over three years later, the thread of comments is still going strong with thousands of responses—the site usually garners only ten or so comments for every "confession." Our anonymous Ann had hit a nerve.

One woman who got pregnant at forty-two wrote, "I hate being a mother too. Every day is the same. And to think I won't be free of it until I am like 60 and then my life will be over." Another, identifying herself only as k'smom, said, "I feel so trapped, anxious and overwhelmed. I love my daughter and she's well taken care of but this is not the path I would have taken given a second chance."

Gianna wrote, "I love my son, but I hate being a mother. It has been a thankless, monotonous, exhausting, irritating and oppressive job. Motherhood feels like a prison sentence. I can't wait until I am paroled when my son turns 18 and hopefully goes far away to college." One DC-based mom even said that although she was against abortion before having her son, now she would "run to the abortion clinic" if she got pregnant again.

The responses—largely from women who identify themselves as financially stable—spell out something less explicit than well-worn reasons for parental unhappiness such as pov-

erty and a lack of support. These women simply don't feel
that motherhood is all it's cracked up to be, and if given a second chance, they wouldn't do it again.

Some cited the boredom of stay-at-home momism. Many
complained of partners who didn't shoulder their share of
child care responsibilities. "Like most men, my husband
doesn't do much—if anything—for baby care. I have to do
and plan for everything," one mother wrote. A few got pregnant accidentally and were pressured by their husbands and
boyfriends to carry through with the pregnancy, or knew
they never wanted children but felt it was something they
"should" do.

The overwhelming sentiment, however, was the feeling of
a loss of self, the terrifying reality that their lives had been
subsumed into the needs of their child. DS wrote, "I feel like
I have completely lost any thing that was me. I never imagined having children and putting myself aside would make
me feel this bad." The expectation of total motherhood is bad
enough, having to live it out every day is soul crushing. Everything that made us an individual, that made us unique, no
longer matters. It's our role as a mother that defines us. Not
much has changed.

"The feminine mystique permits, even encourages, women
to ignore the question of their identity," wrote Betty Friedan.
"The mystique says they can answer the question 'Who am I?'
by saying 'Tom's wife . . . Mary's mother.' The truth is—and
how long it's been true, I'm not sure, but it was true in my
generation and it's true of girls growing up today—an American woman no longer has a private image to tell her who she
is, or can be, or wants to be."

At the time she published *The Feminine Mystique,* Friedan
argued that the public image of women was largely one of do-

mesticity—"washing machines, cake mixes . . . detergents," all sold through commercials and magazines. Today, American women have more public images of themselves than that of a housewife. We see ourselves depicted in television, ads, movies, and magazines (not to mention real life!) as politicians, business owners, intellectuals, soldiers, and more. But that's what makes the public image of total motherhood so insidious. We see these diverse images of ourselves and believe that the oppressive standard Friedan wrote about is dead, when in fact it has simply shifted. Because no matter how many different kinds of public images women see of themselves, they're still limited. They're still largely white, straight upper-middle-class depictions, and they all still identify women as mothers or non-mothers.

American culture can't accept the reality of a woman who does not want to be a mother. It goes against everything we've been taught to think about women and how desperately they want babies. If we're to believe the media and pop culture, women—even teen girls—are forever desperate for a baby. It's our greatest desire.

The truth is, most women spend the majority of their lives trying *not* to get pregnant. According to the Guttmacher Institute,[3] by the time a woman with two children is in her mid-forties she will have spent only five years trying to become pregnant, being pregnant, and not being at risk for getting pregnant following a birth. But to avoid getting pregnant before or after those two births, she would have had to refrain from sex or use contraception for an average of twenty-five years. Almost all American women (99 percent), ages fifteen to forty-four, who have had sexual intercourse use some form of birth control. The second most popular form of birth control after the Pill? Sterilization. And now, more than ever, women are increasingly choosing forms of contraception that are for long-term use. Since 2005, for example, IUD use has increased by a whopping 161 percent. That's a long part of life and a lot of effort to avoid parenthood!

Now, it may be that these statistics simply indicate that modern women are just exerting more control over when and under what circumstances they become mothers. To a large degree that's true. But it's doesn't jibe with an even more shocking reality: that half of pregnancies in the United States are unintended. Once you factor in the abortion rate and pregnancies that end in miscarriage, we're left with the rather surprising fact that one third of babies born in the United States were unplanned. Not so surprising, however, is that the intention to have children definitively impacts how parents feel about their children, and how those children are treated—sometimes to terrifying results.

Jennifer Barber, a population researcher at the University of Michigan, studied more than three thousand mothers[4] and their close to six thousand children from a range of socioeconomic backgrounds. Barber and her colleagues asked women who had recently given birth, "Just before you became pregnant, did you want to become pregnant when you did?" Those who answered yes were categorized as "intended"; those who answered no were then asked, "Did you want a baby but not at that time, or did you want none at all?" Depending on their answer, they were classified as "mistimed" or "unwanted." Over 60 percent of the children studied were reported as planned, almost 30 percent were unplanned ("mistimed"), and 10 percent were unequivocally "unwanted."

The results of Barber's research showed that the children who were unintended—both those who were mistimed and those who were unwanted—got fewer parental resources than those children who were intended. Basically, children who were unplanned didn't get as much emotional and cognitive support as children who were planned—as reported both by the researchers and the mothers themselves. Barber's research looked at things like the number of children's books in the home, and how often a parent read to a child or taught them skills like counting or the alphabet for the "cognitive" aspect. For the "emotional" support rating, they developed a scale measuring the "warmth" and "responsiveness" of the mother, how much time the family spent together, and how much time the father spent with the child. Across the board, children who were wanted got more from their parents than children who weren't. Children who were unplanned were also subject to harsher parenting and more punitive measures than a sibling who was intended.

Barber pointed out that this kind of pattern could be due to parental stress and a lack of patience that's "directed explicitly toward an unwanted child," and that a mistimed or unwanted birth could raise stress levels in the parents' interactions with their other children as well. She also says that in addition to benign emotional neglect, parenting unintended children is also associated with infant health problems and mortality, maternal depression, and sometimes child abuse.

Child abuse rates in the United States are astounding, and we have the highest number of child abuse fatalities in the industrialized world. According to the nonprofit group Every Child Matters,[5] a child dies from abuse or neglect in the United States every five hours. The Children's Bureau at the Department of Health and Human Services reports[6] that in 2010 more than 3.6 million children were subjects of at least one report of child abuse. Over seventeen hundred of those children were killed; the majority of them were murdered by one or both of their biological parents. The age that children are most likely to abused? From birth to one year old.

The most common form of child abuse, however, is neglect—78 percent of abused children experience some form if it. Neglect can include anything from allowing your child to drink and take drugs, to failing to provide necessary medical services, or being inattentive to your child's emotional needs, or unable to provide safe shelter or adequate food. Most parents who are found guilty of neglect have a severe lack of access to resources. They're often poor, and some have their own health and emotional problems or are in abusive relationships. But Barber's research, along with the high number of unwanted and unplanned American children, sheds some light on other, less structural, reasons why parents neglect and sometimes hurt their children.

Picking apart intended or planned parenthood also casts a new light on the way that parental obligations are more nuanced (for better or worse) now than in years past.

The trend of "fatherlessness" in the United States, for example, has long been blamed by social conservatives and mainstream media on everything from feminism to certain socioeconomic groups not getting enough support promoting the roles of men in children's lives. While the cause isn't as clear cut as that, statistics do bear out that there is a serious problem of parental responsibility, both financial and personal, especially as it pertains to men. According to the U.S. Census Bureau,[7] only 41 percent of custodial parents received the full amount of child support owed to them in 2009, and in all, $35.1 billion in support was owed that same year.

According to the National Fatherhood Initiative,[8] nine out of ten parents think there's a "father absence crisis" in the United States, and the government seems to agree. The Department of Health and Human Services has a special project, the National Responsible Fatherhood Clearinghouse, dedicated to getting American dads more involved with their kids. The campaign has a "fatherhood pledge" page and a "dad blog," and it has long partnered with advertising companies to come out with catchy public service announcements such as, "Take the time to be a dad today," for a campaign aimed at African American and Latino fathers. The assumption is that most fathers who are not a major part of their children's lives simply need a bit of encouragement.

But some dads believe that not parenting or shunning financial support for their children is actually a reproductive right. In March 2006, an organization called The National Center for Men (NCM) filed suit in a Michigan district court on behalf of twenty-five-year-old Matt Dubay, a computer technician from Saginaw who didn't want to support a child he "never intended to bring into the world." The organization claimed it wanted to fight for men's rights to make reproductive choices—specifically, to decline the responsibilities of fatherhood in the event of an unintended pregnancy. The organization named the lawsuit "Roe for Men."

In a press release that went out before they filed suit, NCM wrote, "More than three decades ago, *Roe vs. Wade* gave women control of their reproductive lives but nothing in the law changed for men . . . Men are routinely forced to give up control, forced to be financially responsible for choice only women are permitted to make, forced to relinquish reproductive choice as the price of intimacy."

According to Dubay, he had a short relationship with his girlfriend (just about three months), and while he was with her, Dubay says he made it clear that he wasn't ready or willing to be a father. She, he says, assured him that she was unable to get pregnant and that she was on contraception for medical reasons, anyway. After they broke up, however, the woman told Dubay that she was pregnant, that she planned to keep the pregnancy, and that she expected financial support once the child was born.

"She has options, those options are overlooked in men," Dubay told an MSNBC reporter. "We have no choice, we just have to live with whatever the women decide."

For Mel Feit, the director of NCM, the issue is not that Dubay's girlfriend was supposedly dishonest, but that she had a choice and Dubay wasn't allowed one. For Feit, it's simply asking for equality. He has a habit of saying that, "reproductive choice isn't a fundamental right if it's limited to people who have internal reproductive systems."

So Dubay, with the help of Feit, made the legal argument that the Michigan Paternity Act violated Dubay's right to "equal protection" under the Fourteenth Amendment that guarantees that "no state shall . . . deny any person within its jurisdiction the equal protection of the law." Their argument was that by letting women have a legal way to get out of parenthood—abortion—but denying that same right to fathers, Dubay's right to equal protection was violated.

The court, however, did not agree. A judge dismissed the case in July 2006 and ordered Dubay to pay child support, as well as the legal fees for his ex-girlfriend and the state of Michigan. A U.S. Court of Appeals then held up the state's decision in late 2007, noting that his case lacked merit and that it is "not a fundamental right of any parent, male of female, to sever his or her financial responsibilities to the child after the child is born." The court also dismissed the idea that a woman's right to abortion is similar to a man's right to decline parenthood, nothing that, "in the case of a father seek-

ing to opt out of fatherhood and thereby avoid child support obligations, the child is already in existence and the state
therefore has an important interest in providing for his or her
support."

In response to the loss, Feit wanted to take Dubay's case to
the Supreme Court, but the young man had had enough. Un-
deterred, Feit found a new plaintiff. Greg Bruell was a more
compelling case for NCM because although he wanted to
fight for the right to not support an unintended child (one he
had with a girlfriend after he divorced his wife), he was also a
stay-at-home dad to his son and daughter. He told a reporter
at *Elle* magazine, "I'm perfectly willing to take the responsibility of raising a child if it's my choice . . . if it's compul-
sory, it becomes impossible."[9] But, as with Dubay, time took
its toll, and Bruell slowly mended his relationship with his ex
and went on to voluntarily support his daughter.

Today, Feit's cause seems dead in the water. While the
courts have ignored his "Roe for Men," Feit pushes the idea
that couples should sign a contract before having sex that
would dictate what they would do should a pregnancy occur.
Such a document wouldn't be legally binding, but Feit con-
siders it a "symbolic protest" against the injustice.

Others who want to renege on parental responsibilities—those who decide to go through adoption "disrup-
tions"—don't face quite the same legal hurdles as men like
Bruell and Dubay, though they do face the same stigma.
When Torry Hansen of Shelbyville, Tennessee, sent her seven-
year-old adopted son by himself on a plane back to his home
country of Russia with nothing more than a note explaining
she didn't want to parent him, she became one of the most re-
viled women in America. Russian officials were so incensed
that they temporarily halted all adoptions to the United

States. We somewhat expect fathers, it seems, to shirk their responsibility. But when mothers do it, it shakes the core of what we've been taught to believe about women and maternal instinct.

Anthropologist Sarah Blaffer Hrdy argued in a 2001 Utah lecture, for example, that being female is seen as synonymous with having and nurturing as many children as possible. So when mothers abandon their children, it's seen as unnatural. This simplistic, emotional response to parents—mothers, in particular—who give up their kids is part of the reason Americans have such a difficult time dealing with the issue. As Hrdy says, "No amount of legislation can ensure that mothers will love their babies."

That's why programs like safe haven laws—age limitations or not—will never truly get to the heart of the matter. As Mary Lee Allen, director of the Children's Defense Fund's child welfare and mental health division, has said, "These laws help women to drop their babies off but do nothing to provide supports to women and children before this happens."[10]

Unfortunately, discussing the structural issues has never been an American strong suit. Hrdy notes that legislators are too afraid to focus on sensible solutions. "Talking about the source of the problem would require policymakers to discuss sex education and contraception, not to mention abortion, and they view even nonsensical social policies as preferable to the prospect of political suicide."

If policymakers and people who care about children want to reduce the number of abandoned kids, they need to address the systemic issues: poverty, maternity leave, access to resources, and health care. We need to encourage women to demand more help from their partners, if they have them. In a way, that's the easier fix, because we know what we have to do there; the issues have been the same for years. The less-obvious hurdle is that of preparing parents emotionally and putting forward realistic images of parenthood and motherhood. There also needs to be some sort of acknowledgment that not everyone should parent—when parenting is a given, it's not fully considered or thought out, and it gives way too easily to parental ambivalence and unhappiness.

Take Trinity, one of the mothers who commented on the Secret Confessions board about hating parenthood. She wrote, "My pregnancy was totally planned and I thought it was a good idea at the time. Nobody tells you the negatives before you get pregnant—they convince you it's a wonderful idea and you will love it. I think it's a secret shared among parents . . . they're miserable so they want you to be too."

By having more honest conversations about parenting, we can avoid the kind of secret depressions so many mothers seem to be harboring. If what we want is deliberate, thought-out, planned, and expected parenthood—and parenting that is healthy and happy for children—then we have to speak out.

EIGHT

"Bad" Mothers Go to Jail

There are no perfect parents . . . just as
there are no perfect children.

— *Mister Rogers*

O N APRIL 10, 2010, thirty-year-old Raquel Nelson took
her three children out for pizza for a family birthday
party. Nelson, a single mother, also stopped with her
kids at a Walmart before taking a bus to get back home. After
getting off the bus, Nelson noticed that they had missed their
transfer and the next bus wouldn't arrive for another hour.
Her apartment building was right across the street—a divided
highway—so she and other passengers from the bus started
to cross the lanes to get home. At one of the medians, Nelson's son, four-year-old A.J., ran into the road. Nelson ran after him—she, her son, and her two-year-old daughter were
hit by a van. The driver left the scene; Nelson and her daughter were injured, A.J. was killed.

Just weeks after the accident, the police came to Nelson's

home and arrested her. She was charged with second-degree vehicular homicide, failing to cross at a crosswalk, and reckless conduct. In July 2011, a jury found Nelson guilty of the manslaughter and reckless endangerment charges; the grieving mother faced three years in prison. The driver of the van that hit Nelson and her children, Jerry Guy, had two hit-and-run convictions and confessed to drinking the day of the accident. He pleaded guilty, was sentenced to five years in prison, but served only six months. So at the time of her conviction, Nelson faced more jail time than the drunk driver who killed her son—all because she didn't cross the street at a crosswalk.

We've moved beyond simple social pressure to be the perfect mom. Today, if you fall short as a parent you can be arrested for it. Nelson's story is shocking, but it's not unique. American culture and politics holds a certain disdain for those women who have been deemed "bad" mothers—from the overzealous prosecution of parents to our national obsession with teen mothers and "pageant moms." Part of the search for ideal parenting is being able to identify those parents who supposedly don't measure up—and punishing them for it.

In *"Bad" Mothers: The Politics of Blame in Twentieth-Century America*, history professors Molly Ladd-Taylor and Lauri Umansky take on this culture of mother-punishment, noting that "the label of 'bad' mother has been applied for far more women than whose actions would warrant the name."

They point out the long history of blaming mothers for things out of their control. For example, in the 1920s, spicy and garlicky food that immigrant women fed to their babies was thought to be a major factor in infant mortality. Up until the 1950s, overprotective mothers were thought to be the cause of homosexuality in boys, and aloof "refrigerator" mothers were believed to cause disorders we now know as autism and schizophrenia.

As infant mortality started to drop, parents and experts began to blame children's death and illnesses on their environment more and more. "Infant death was preventable—if the mother kept her home clean and sanitary and followed the experts' advice. With the improvements in infant health and the rise of such professions as psychology and medical pediatric, the experts' attention moved from physical health to mental development. The shift had dire consequences for the mother," they wrote.

And as the culture changed, so did the intensity by which we blamed mothers. As professional child development experts rose to prominence and gender roles changed—thanks in large part to the feminist movement—the belief that children's development, health, and wellness were based entirely on what mothers did or didn't do became culturally ingrained.

Today, this expectation of perfect motherhood—and the punishment that goes along with transgressing—starts before women even become parents.

MURDER BY MOTHERING

In January 2004, Melissa Ann Rowland, a twenty-eight-year-old woman from West Jordan, Utah, was charged with criminal homicide after she refused a C-section and gave birth to twins, one of which was stillborn. According to court documents, Rowland sought medical attention because she couldn't feel her twins moving. After examining her, a doctor at LDS Hospital in Salt Lake City recommended that she have C-section immediately—her amniotic fluid was low

and the fetuses' heart rates were low. Rowland, who is mentally ill, refused and left the hospital. She told a nurse that she
didn't want the procedure because she was afraid the doctors
would cut her "from breast bone to pubic bone." Less than
two weeks later, Rowland showed up at another hospital in
labor where she finally agreed to a C-section. Rowland delivered a boy and a girl—the boy was stillborn.

Rowland is hardly the poster child for good motherhood.
She had been previously convicted of child abuse after she
punched her daughter in a supermarket and admitted to using drugs while pregnant. But the reason she was arrested and
charged was specifically because she refused the C-section.
Katha Pollitt, a columnist for *The Nation,* wrote[1] of the case,
"[T]he point at issue in the murder charge remained whether
pregnant women are people or vessels: Can they decide what
is done to their bodies, what risks to take, or not? And what's
next? Will women who miscarry or whose babies are born
dead or sickly be jailed for smoking or drinking during pregnancy? For failing to follow doctor's orders on diet or bed rest?
For choosing a home birth?"

The slippery slope that Rebecca Kukla is worried about
concerning the "pre-pregnant" movement is already in play,
punishing women for failing to be good mothers before
their babies are even born. Iowa considered passing a law
that would make smoking while pregnant a prosecutable of-
fense; in 2010 the state arrested a pregnant woman after she
fell down a flight of stairs for attempting to kill her fetus even
though there was no evidence to that effect. In 2005 a Virginia
lawmaker tried to pass a bill that would mandate women who
had miscarriages to report it to the police within twelve hours
or face up to a year in jail. In 2011 a bill proposed in Geor-
gia required all miscarriages be investigated by police to make

sure they weren't caused by any "human involvement." And in 2010, Utah legislators tried to pass a bill that would allow life sentences for women who have miscarriages after "reckless" behavior. After vocal opposition, legislators changed the bill to say that only women who commit "knowing" acts that result in stillbirths or miscarriages would be prosecuted. But the deliberately vague language put all pregnant women in Utah in danger. Lynn Paltrow, executive director of the National Advocates for Pregnant Women, wrote about the bill for *The Huffington Post*:[2]

> What does this mean? Under this bill, pregnant women who "know" that their cancer medications or other prescription medications could risk harm or cause pregnancy loss could still be arrested. Pregnant women who stay with abusive husbands who they "know" to be angry about the pregnancy could still be arrested under this law. Pregnant women who continue working in jobs they "know" pose hazards to their pregnancies could still be arrested under the law.

Paltrow, who frequently defends pregnant women who have been arrested under these sketchy and often arcane laws, told me that certain legislation—from "fetal protection" laws to anti-abortion "personhood" legislation—has made pregnant women second-class citizens in the United States. "They are establishing precedent that would denaturalize pregnant women," she says.

When Texas enacted a prenatal protection law, for example, a local district attorney sent a letter to every hospital in his jurisdiction demanding that they turn over their records on pregnant women. He told hospital administrations that the records had to be released since the DA's office was now free to prosecute women for doing anything that could be seen as endangering their fetuses; forty women were subsequently arrested.

I first met Paltrow at a conference she organized in 2007—the National Summit to Ensure the Health and Humanity of Pregnant Women. It was there that I heard Laura Pemberton, and there that I realized Paltrow's warnings about pregnant women's rights and punitive measures for "bad" mothers were scarily on the mark. Pemberton, who roamed the conference hall with her children in tow dressed in matching clothing, told this audience of mostly pro-choice activists about being pro-life and religious, but because of an experience she had in 1996, she supported Paltrow's and other pro-choicers' efforts to overturn fetal protection laws.

Pemberton, who was living in Florida at the time, had a C-section a year earlier, in 1995, that she had consented to for the health of the fetus. With the next pregnancy, however, she wanted to give birth vaginally. She couldn't find a doctor who would agree to take her on—many doctors are hesitant to attend a VBAC (vaginal birth after C-section). So after doing some research and finding a midwife, Pemberton decided with her family that she would give birth at home. When her labor started, everything went smoothly. At one point, however, she became dehydrated and decided to go to the hospital to get IV fluids.

The nurses and resident doctor examined Pemberton and told her everything looked normal. However, when the attending doctor realized that Pemberton was attempting a VBAC, she refused to give her an IV unless she would sign a consent form to get a C-section. Pemberton asked what would happen if she signed the consent form, got the IV, but then changed her mind about the surgery. The doctor replied that the hospital would get a court order mandating the C-section. At this point, a sympathetic nurse who had been caring for Pemberton told her that there was chaos in the hallways: The hospital administrator had become involved, the hospital lawyers had been contacted, and they were attempting to get a court order. The nurse suggested that if Pemberton wanted to give birth vaginally, she should leave the hospital through the back door—and fast.

So Pemberton, fully in labor, hurriedly got dressed—so fearful that she would be forced to have a C-section that she didn't take the time to put her shoes on—and rushed down two flights of stairs in the back of the hospital while in active labor.

Once home, Pemberton said she felt safe and "away from the chaos." But soon after, the deputy sheriff and state attorney arrived at Pemberton's house and literally walked into the bedroom in which she was laboring.

"I begged the state attorney not to take me," she said. "I felt sure I couldn't be forced out of my own home." She started squatting in desperation, hoping to get her baby into her vaginal canal so that they couldn't forcibly take her. But the state attorney told Pemberton that a judge had issued a court order and that she would be going to the hospital.

"I couldn't believe what was happening—there's no way that anyone has this right. Was this a nightmare?" As Pemberton attempted to get dressed, an EMT and the state attorney followed her wherever she went, fearing she would flee. They then put her on a stretcher, strapped her arms and legs down, and took her away in an ambulance.

"I felt total humiliation and I knew in my heart what was happening to me was wrong," she said. Once again, while Pemberton was in her hospital room bathroom changing, she tried to get her baby out—she could feel the head with her hand, yet officials still wouldn't allow her to continue to labor naturally. Two doctors, a sheriff, two attorneys, and a judge came into her room to have a trial right then and there. (A lawyer had been appointed for her fetus—none was provided to Pemberton.)

"My desire to labor and give birth naturally was not just a religious one, but an informed one," Pemberton told the audience—but the judge had made up his mind. He told her that her unborn child was in control of the state and that it was the state's responsibility to bring the baby into the world safely. As she was wheeled into surgery, she once again refused to sign the consent form. Pemberton said she felt like she was raped by the system and the state.

Later, when Pemberton sued for civil rights violations, a U.S. District Court in Florida ruled that, "whatever the scope of Ms. Pemberton's personal constitutional rights in this situation, they clearly did not outweigh the interests of the State of Florida in preserving the life of the unborn child."

This "interests of the State" in children—even unborn children—manifests in the United States in ways much more punitive than preventative. For Pemberton, it meant forced surgery—a violation of bodily integrity if there ever was one. Florida took away her right not just to be a mother making a decision for her child, but to be a person making a decision about her own health and safety. For others, it can mean that even when they follow social cues for how to be a "good" mom, they can still be punished.

Take thirty-seven-year-old Stephanie Greene of Campobello, South Carolina.[3] She's being charged with murdering her newborn daughter, Alexis, in 2010. Prosecutors allege that she killed her five-week-old baby by *breastfeeding* her—the very thing American moms are encouraged, even pressured, to do. Prosecutors in South Carolina say that Greene's breast milk contained deadly amounts of morphine, and that Alexis died of an overdose. Greene takes opioids for pain and high blood pressure that resulted from a car accident. She didn't tell the hospital where she delivered that she was taking the medication because South Carolina has a history of prosecuting pregnant women who use drugs, even if they are legal and prescribed by a doctor. After Greene brought her daughter home, however, she told a hospital lactation consultant about her medications; the consultant pointed her in the direction of a government website that lists drugs and their safety during breastfeeding. The site listed morphine as safe for nursing mothers, as does the La Leche League. (Many women—especially those who have had C-sections—take pain killers in the days and weeks after giving birth and breastfeed their babies.)

Before Alexis died, she had a cold—Greene was keeping her pediatrician updated by phone. In the middle of the night, however, Alexis's father, Randy, noticed that the baby was cold and not breathing. Greene gave infant CPR and Randy called 911 but by the time paramedics arrived, Alexis had died. Nine months later, Green was arrested for using morphine while breastfeeding. She's awaiting trial and isn't allowed to be alone with her three children.

Emily Horowitz, a professor of sociology and criminal justice at St. Francis College in New York, studies media coverage of crimes, false convictions, and the problems faced by incarcerated women. She wrote of Greene's case, "The idea of a mother taking drugs and breastfeeding causes outrage, and if a baby with a drug-using mother dies this only increases[4] moral panic and demands for justice. . . . The moral panic about adults deliberately harming children in their care is an unfortunate reality of modern times."

Horowitz also pointed out that some moms are more at risk for scrutiny than others—the more marginalized a mother, the more likely she is to be considered "suspect" as a parent. Raquel Nelson, for example—who is black—was convicted by an all-white jury. (After an outcry by racial justice groups, her sentence was changed to probation and community service—she is seeking a new trial.) Mothers of color and low-income moms are more likely to be drug-tested at hospitals, investigated by child services, and reported for "suspicious" parenting behavior.

In 2002, a mother in Meriden, Connecticut, was arrested and eventually convicted of risk of injury to a minor. Why? Her twelve-year-old son committed suicide and the state said she didn't do enough to get him help. Daniel Scruggs was a troubled kid—he wore strange clothes, didn't bathe often, and would sometimes soil himself at school. Not so surprisingly, he was also the victim of intense bullying, something experts say was a major factor in his suicide. Police said his mother, Judith Scruggs, kept the house in disarray and never did anything to ensure that her son got the medical and psychological help he obviously so desperately needed. But Scruggs lacked the time and financial resources to be able to fully care for Daniel; she worked seventy hours a week at two jobs—one at Walmart, one as a teacher's aide. Her lawyer told *ABC News* in 2002, "Under her contract with the school, she could not be late . . . and when you're holding down two jobs and you're the sole supporter of two children, every single penny counts." Scruggs's conviction was overturned in 2006.

Mothers of color or low-income women are considered "bad" even when they do things that are par for the course for "good" (white, upper middle class) mothers, and are likely to be punished because of their race or class.

In 2009, Kelley Williams-Bolar,[5] a forty-year-old, black, single mother of two, was arrested for sending her kids to school in the wrong school district. Williams-Bolar, who lives in a housing project in Akron, Ohio, and works as a teaching assistant for special-needs children, sent her daughters to school in a better neighborhood by using her father's home address as her residence. Gaming the educational system is hardly new, and it's something that white upper-middle-class parents do frequently and with impunity. But when Ohio officials found out that Williams-Bolar's children didn't live with their grandfather, they ordered her to pay over thirty thousand dollars in "back tuition." When Williams-Bolar couldn't pay, she was charged with grand theft and sentenced to five years in prison. Her father was also charged. After activist groups expressed outrage, her sentence was reduced to ten days in jail, but both Williams-Bolar and her father still face felony charges of tampering with records.

Similarly in 2011, Tanya McDowell,[6] a black, single mother who was homeless in Bridgeport, Connecticut, used her babysitter's address to register her five-year-old son in kindergarten in a better school district of Norwalk. McDowell is facing twenty years in prison and a fifteen-thousand-dollar fine—all for trying to provide the best education possible for her child.

So what does it take to be a "good" mother? Anything less than total commitment, a complete negation of self, won't do. That's why American culture still venerates mothers-as-martyrs. Women who give up their lives to save their children—especially their unborn children—are held up as the ideal parent. Take Stacey Crimm. She was diagnosed with[7] cancer while pregnant, she refused chemotherapy, and subsequently died after an emergency C-section saved her two-pound daughter. Her story is the latest in what one headline called, "A Mother's Ultimate Gift."

Seventeen-year-old Jenni Lake of Idaho had a similar story. Just two week after she found out she had cancer, she discovered she was ten weeks pregnant. She decided to forgo cancer treatment, and died twelve days after delivering a boy. She reportedly told a nurse, "I'm done, I did what I was supposed to do. My baby is going to get here safe."[8]

The best kind of mother is one who gives up her life—literally—for her child. There could be no clearer, or more disturbing, message. If we want to be good mothers, we need to give up ourselves—whether it's our freedom, or sense of self, our careers, even our lives. It's this expectation, this cruel and unusual standard, that drives too many American mothers to beat themselves up over the ways in which they do not hold up to an impossible standard, and which punishes, bizarrely, women who stray too far from that ideal.

NINE

Smart Women Don't Have Kids

> Could these childless women be harbingers of a new
> world, one in which parenthood is considered an active
> choice and not simply the default state of adulthood?
> Perhaps future generations will look at phenomena like
> the Jennifer Aniston tabloid womb obsession and wonder
> how it was possible that anyone could have once cared
> so much if some women chose not to have babies.
>
> — *Amanda Marcotte, Slate*[1]

IN 2010, A STUDY from the Pew Research Center[2] showed
that the rate of American women who did not have children had almost doubled since 1976. That's nearly one
in five women today, compared with one in ten thirty years
ago. The study also showed that American attitudes toward
women choosing not to have children have become more accepting than in years past, and most people disagreed that
people without children "lead empty lives"—yet a significant
percentage, 41 percent, agreed with the sentiment. In a 2009
survey, 38 percent of Americans said that they felt the child-

lessness trend was "bad for society," up almost 10 percent from a survey just two years earlier.

Though the United States is making progress in terms of seeing women as more than just the sum of their reproductive parts, the stigma surrounding childlessness is still alive and well. Women who don't have children are still largely viewed as an anomaly at best, and at worst, sad and selfish. But stigma aside, they sure do seem to be having a good time.

Robin Simon, a sociology professor at Florida State University and researcher on parenting and happiness, told *The Daily Beast* in 2008[3] that parents "experience lower levels of emotional well-being, less frequent positive emotions and more frequent negative emotions than their childless peers. In fact, no group of parents—married, single, step, or even empty nest—reported significantly greater emotional well-being than people who never had children," she said. "It's such a counterintuitive finding because we have these cultural beliefs that children are the key to happiness and a healthy life, and they're not."

Perhaps it's time to ask: Do women who don't have children know something that parents don't?

Laura Scott, author of *Two Is Enough: A Couple's Guide to Living Childless by Choice,* says that the number one reason women cite for not wanting to have children is not wanting their life to change. Scott conducted a study over the course of two years of child-free women. (Many prefer to call themselves "child-free" as opposed to "childless" as the latter implies an absence or void of something whereas "child-free" is a more positive term.) Of the respondents, 74 percent said they "had no desire to have a child, no maternal instinct." Other reasons given for not wanting children: loving the relationship they were in "as it is," valuing "freedom and indepen-

dence," not wanting to take on the responsibility of raising a
child, the desire to focus time and energy "on my own interests, needs and goals," and wanting to accomplish "things in
life that would be difficult to do if I was a parent."

"Parenting is no longer the default," Scott told me. "For
a lot of people it's no longer an assumption—it's a decision.
There's a trend of the intentional postponement of childbearing for women and men in the United States."

Scott says she started the survey as part of her own personal journey, after she had decided not to have children and
had to deal with an onslaught of criticism. "Everyone told me
I was going to change my mind, that once I was in my thirties
that I would want children. But that never happened for me,"
she said. "I wanted to know—and understand why—that
was, and if there were other men and women who simply
didn't have the desire to have children."

And that's what was missing from the Pew study—the research that they *didn't* do, examining childlessness rates among
men. Parenting is still thought of as a specifically female endeavor, and despite the fact that both men and women choose
not to have children, Americans still focus entirely on wom-
en's decisions around parenting.

One of the things Scott was most surprised to find in her
research was how many men were actively seeking out a child-
free life—she says quite a few men she spoke to had vasecto-
mies in their twenties. Women, on the other hand, had a difficult time finding doctors who would perform the procedure
without the women going to counseling or therapy first. Scott
also says that women got more push back when telling friends
and family that they didn't want to have children.

"There seems to be an assumption that women are in-
nately maternal and desire children and that men are less so."

For men who had made the decision not to have children, the skepticism most often took the form of curiosity and concern that the men wouldn't find partners who also didn't want kids. Scott also noted that a lot of the men got more positive responses from parents than did women. They were told things like, "You're right not to have kids—it's really difficult." Women, however, did not get this kind of validation.

Scott says the fact that so much research focuses solely on women ignores the reality that parenting is "trending towards a co-parenting model."

"We can't assume that women are the primary caregiver," Scott says. "We need to challenge the idea that women are inherently maternal or biologically driven to have children."

Biology aside, it's still women who do the majority of parenting and caretaking, and it's women whose lives change the most when a child comes along. We're the ones who are more likely to take time off from work, if we don't stop working entirely; we're the ones who do the majority of the domestic work, care work, mental work (are there enough diapers? when was his last doctor's appointment?); and women are more likely to pay the economic price of having a family.

Dr. Tanya Koropeckyj-Cox, a sociology professor at the University of Florida, has said[4] that some women may not have children because of the inequality around men and women's roles in child rearing. "Studies have documented that men tend to experience pretty strong economic and social rewards from being a dad, whereas women experience more of the pressures and more of the demands of the immediate day-to-day reality of parenting and juggling work," she said.

This differing experience of pressure and demands may be, in part, why the majority of women who choose not to have children are among the most highly educated and successful in the country. The 2010 Pew report showed that the most educated women are still the most likely group in the United States to never have had a child: in 2008, 24 percent of women ages forty to forty-four with a professional (i.e., medical or legal), master's, or doctoral degree had not had children. The rates among those groups were similar — 25 percent of women with a master's degree and 23 percent of women with a doctorate or professional degree had never had children.

Nancy Folbre, an economics professor at the University of Massachusetts in Amherst, wrote in *The New York Times*[5] that higher education can provide access to more flexible jobs, and women in professional or managerial jobs who do have children are more likely than other working mothers to reduce their work hours when they have a young child. But higher degrees can also mean a higher level of success level at work, and with more responsibilities in public life, domestic duties or choices can be overwhelming. That may be one of the reasons why women who are high up on the corporate ladder, or in public service, are more likely to be child free — in part by choice, but also by circumstance. Koropeckyj-Cox speculated that some women might choose to forgo motherhood because of the burden of how difficult the dual roles of mother and working woman are.

A 2010 study out of the University of Chicago[6] that looked at business school graduates and their career trajectories, for example, showed that women were much more likely to take time off than their male counterparts. Women took time off or worked part time mostly to care for children; as a result, fifteen years after graduating, the men in the study were making 75 percent more money than the women. The only group of women who had similar careers to that of the men in the study was women who never had children.

The study's authors wrote, "The presence of children is the main contributor to the lesser job experience, greater career discontinuity, and shorter work hours for female MBAs. Across the first 15 years following the MBA, women with children have about an 8 month deficit in actual post-MBA experience compared with the average man, while women without children have a 1.5 month deficit." They also found that women with children generally worked 24 percent fewer weekly hours than men, while women without children worked only 3 percent fewer hours.

Response to the study—and the assumption that its data meant mothers were less likely to succeed—was mixed. The organization Catalyst,[7] whose mission is to advance women's roles in business and the workplace, pointed to their own study, "Women and Men in U.S. Corporate Leadership," which showed that most senior-level employees were married and have children. They also pointed out that of the fourteen female *Fortune 500* CEOs, twelve have children.

"Blaming inequity on factors like motherhood obscures a simple truth: entrenched biases and sexist stereotypes impact *all* women," Catalyst wrote in a statement. "Misrepresenting this reality doesn't solve the problem. It distracts all of us—including employers who lose out on great talent—from addressing core inequity." I don't think anyone would disagree that all women face sexism in the workplace, but the data on mothers and women without children is hard to ignore.

Kristin Rowe-Finkbeiner, executive director of MomsRising.org, has long pointed out that the maternal pay gap is all too real: Women who don't have children make 90 cents to a man's dollar; women with children make 73 cents to that dollar. And let's not forget the study out of Cornell that showed that a woman without children is twice as likely to be hired as a mother with the same résumé—and is offered eleven thousand dollars more in starting salary.

Women with children also suffer in the workplace in distinct ways that men do not. Male parents who work often have a wife (either at home or at work) who does the bulk of child care. This support at home frees men up to work more hours and to network outside of work and after-work hours—golf games, happy hours, and racquetball abound. For women with children at home, however, it's incredibly rare that they have similar support from their husbands.

American women with children have the "second shift" at home—filled with child care, housework, and domestic responsibilities beyond their work outside the home. Arlie Hochschild introduced the idea of these extra work hours in her 1989 best-selling book, *The Second Shift: Working Parents and the Revolution at Home.* Hochschild—whose ideas still hold true today, sadly—wrote that women are dealing with a "stalled revolution." When women got out of the home and into the workplace, their domestic responsibilities were not erased but simply moved to after-work hours. She argued that women's jobs are seen as jobs, while husbands' are seen as careers; so women's paid work is devalued and seen as the more expendable career in the relationship.

This disparity is not lost on women—who may decide that in order to succeed, they need to forgo or stall having children. It may also explain why women tend to be more accepting of childlessness than men—they understand why for some women, trying to "do it all" in an unjust system isn't going to cut it.

Koropeckyj-Cox's research on attitudes toward child-free women, published in the *Journal of Marriage and Family,* indicates that women are generally more comfortable with the idea of not having children than men are. Her study, based on research collected in two large-scale national studies, showed that, "on a basic level, for men and women, parenting and parenthood mean different things. The responses indicate greater acceptance of childlessness, particularly among women, as one possible life path whether chosen or shaped by circumstances." Perhaps women understand the downsides and sacrifices of having children in a way that men do not. Even in the most equal of relationships, something shifts when children are brought into the picture—particularly for straight couples.

Blue Milk blogger Andie Fox says that because she had such an equal partnership with the man who would become the father of her children, the inequality that manifested once they had children was a tremendous—and unwelcomed—surprise. "It's such a shock when you try and sort out equality in your relationship—and this is with a man who *wants* to be more equal and wants to be more fair. Yet we still slip constantly into unequal and traditional divisions of work," she told me.

Fox, who is the only mother at her workplace, says, "I think there's such incredible obstacles for mothers in terms of integrating their mothering roles with their workplaces; this kind of tension is unsustainable, we're going to have to move forward. We'll look back in a hundred years' time and think it's ridiculous."

For some women, it's not just the inequality at home or at work that influences their decision to not have children, but the inequality of the country in general. Activist and writer Melissa McEwan has written[8] that she has never wanted children, but it's become clearer to her as she's gotten older that this decision also comes from seeing the way that women and mothers are treated by society and sexist politics. She points to the assault on women's reproductive rights—based in the idea that all women should be mothers, even if by force—as something that has shaped her decision making. She writes,

> I don't want children, because I so dearly want a choice, because I so ardently want autonomy, because I so desperately want my full humanity. I have understood, intuitively, from a very early age that, in this culture, in the spaces in which I move, to have children is to dilute one's value as a human, even as it is to enhance one's value as a woman. For the first time, I consider the possibility that I don't even really know if I want children or don't want them. All I know with certainty is that I will not have them. Not like this.

But why look into reasons women decide not to have children at all? Why the need for explanation? After all, people rarely ask parents why they chose to have children—it would be considered odd, and a bit rude. But when it comes to women without children, asking about their private life and relationship is seen as perfectly socially acceptable.

Lisa Hymas, the editor of an environmental blog, wrote that her decision not to have children was in part because of her green politics, but also because of what she would be missing out on. "Parents miss out on a lot:[9] time and emotional energy to invest in friendships and a romantic partnership. Space to focus on a career or education or avocation. Travel that's truly impulsive or leisurely or adventurous, eight peaceful, uninterrupted hours of sleep a night. Sunday brunches out!"

Though Hymas's decision was based on carefully thought out personal and political reasons, she still gets hounded about her choice not to have children.

On forums for women without children (I have yet to see such a space for child-free men), the most talked about topic is the need to constantly justify their decision, something mothers never have to do. The criticisms are so common that contributors on child-free sites refer to the steady and predictable line of questioning of their choice as "breeder bingo." (As in, you can fill in a bingo card of all the lines you hear: "Children are our future!" "Don't you want to give your parents grandchildren?")

You need only to look at media headlines to see why they're so defensive. A *Today* show segment asks, "Is it wrong for a woman not to want to have children?" An MSN headline reads, "Is Being Child-Free by Choice Selfish?"

On a forum, The Childfree Life, Annabelle86, who lives in the Great Lakes area of Pennsylvania, says that people in her region "expect you to change your mind." She writes,

> Most of the girls I graduated with are popping out [kids] left and right and when I state my CF [child free] status, I feel like people pat me on the head and tell me I am young and will change my mind. When I decided to get a TL [tubal ligation] there was a panic to convince me to change my mind, but I am very tired of people not taking my choice seriously. If other 25 year olds are old enough to make the permanent life choice of having kids, I am damn sure old enough to decide I never want them.

Another poster, JessicaWabbit from Virginia, wrote that she mostly gets confused faces when she tells people she doesn't want children. "I suppose it never occurred to them that having kids is a choice."

And that's the issue that Laura Scott, author of *Two Is Enough*, says she finds truly disturbing: that she often speaks to women that say they didn't know that they had a choice. "I see this a lot—where women are feeling a lot of external pressure and not owning feelings of ambivalence around having children," she told me. Many of these women—like the mothers who ended up on the anonymous board talking about how much they hated parenthood—end up profoundly unhappy.

"We've all seen people who have had kids who weren't planned and who aren't prepared for the parenthood role—then they have feelings of self blame of being a terrible mother and beating themselves up."

The intention to have children directly impacts parental happiness and the way that parents treat children—yet that conversation still remains taboo. "There's a disconnect—we don't challenge those who do have children about how wise that decision was, but people who don't have children are constantly questioned about the wisdom of their decision," says Scott.

Given the reality of unintended parenthood and parental unhappiness, one would think that women and men who make the decision not to have children—who are deliberate and thoughtful about the choice to bring another person into the world—would be seen as less selfish than those who unthinkingly have children. Yet the stigma remains.

Scott, for one, is hopeful. She believes there's more support for intentional decision making around parenthood than there was twenty years ago. "We can all agree that intentional parenthood will lead to a better outcome than unintentional parenthood."

The Pew study bears some of that optimism out. In 1990, 65 percent of people said they believed children were essential for a good marriage; today only 40 percent think as much.

Additionally, 46 percent of the public says it makes no difference in terms of societal impact if women do not ever have
children. So perhaps the tide is turning. "What I'm hoping is
that we recognize that we do have a choice and we recognize
that no matter what you choose, it's entirely possible to have a
fulfilling, rich, and purposeful life," says Scott.

Public skepticism or acceptance aside, women—and
men!—choosing not to have children is here to stay, and posi-
tioning parenthood as the default instead of a deliberate deci-
sion-making process is not only shortsighted but harmful.

TEN

Death of the Nuclear Family

I sustain myself with the love of family.
— *Maya Angelou*

A dysfunctional family is any family with
more than one person in it.
— *Mary Karr, The Liars' Club*

W HEN REBEKAH SPICUGLIA got pregnant at seventeen, she says abortion wasn't an option. "I was raised by a fanatically religious family. I probably considered adoption briefly." Her boyfriend was a new one, and it was the first sexual relationship she had been involved in. So Spicuglia moved in with her boyfriend, and ten days after giving birth to her son, Oscar, they got married.

Spicuglia's marriage didn't last long; she says they were very different people. After he came back from a trip to Mexico she says there was a rift between them. So she moved from their home in Santa Maria, California, to go to college at the University of California at Berkeley. Up until then, their parenting responsibilities had been quite equal, she says. Oscar lived with her, but her ex was always involved and had even traveled for several months in Mexico with Oscar. So when she moved to Berkeley, it didn't faze her to make a verbal agreement that Oscar would stay in Santa Maria with his father and his father's family until Spicuglia secured family housing.

But it took a long time for her name to come up in the family-housing lottery. "I was in school full time, working thirty hours a week, and was four hours away from home," Spicuglia told me. Because she had to work on the weekends at a restaurant, she was able to see Oscar only about once a month. She says it was odd: "I felt like a parent, but I didn't look like a parent to anyone around me." By the time Spicuglia finally got family housing, it was over a year later.

When she told her ex that she was ready for Oscar to come live with her, he said no. "He told me that he loved him and felt he could take better care of him since I would be in school and he had extended family there." He also told Spicuglia that he wouldn't let her see Oscar until she agreed to this custody arrangement. "I realized that I had no power in this situation—our agreement was verbal and he had been living with his dad for a year," she says. "I had no family or financial support, legal resources—I didn't know where to begin." Spicuglia realized that if she wanted to fight for Oscar, she would have to drop out of school. She also had no money for a lawyer. She was devastated.

"But the logical part of me was wondering, *Is his dad right?*" With his father, Oscar had a big family in town and he was happy and stable. Spicuglia says she felt conflicted about uprooting him. "I wasn't going to put his dad through family court and spend thousands of dollars—and put Oscar through that—just because I want my son," she says. "It felt really selfish."

After ceding custody of her son to her ex-husband, and once Spicuglia graduated, she moved to New York City for work. Today Spicuglia, now thirty-three years old, says that her noncustodial arrangement with her ex is working out. "My son is better traveled than everyone in his class; he's been to New York, San Francisco, Paris, Mexico," she says.

"It's hard, but my father raised me with the belief that you're a better role model for your children if you follow your dreams and goals—and Oscar is happy and safe." Spicuglia is on good terms with her ex, and has joint legal custody of her son, meaning she's equally involved in decision making for Oscar's care.

Recently Spicuglia began talking publicly about her life as a noncustodial mom. She wrote articles, and appeared in a spread in *Marie Claire* under the somewhat unfortunate headline, "What Kind of Mother Leaves her Kids?"[1] Before, she had been worried about what people would say. "As a society, we have this idea that if you don't live with your kids it's assumed that you're not a good mother, that you don't love them, you don't want them, or you can't care for them," she says. "Fathers face their own issues, of course—but they're expected not to have custody." Spicuglia now runs a NYC-based group for noncustodial parents as well as a blog and online community where people from around the country, mothers especially, share their stories.

Malinda Temple wrote in, for example, the day she became a noncustodial mother to her two children, five and three years old. She writes that she has been a stay-at-home mom since their birth and since making her decision has heard numerous angry remarks from family, friends and acquaintances. When we separated, my two children and I moved in with my parents with no car and no income. Having not worked outside the home in 8 years, finding a job was increasingly difficult—I had become an emotional wreck, completely unable to support my children, financially or emotionally. My ex-husband was able to financially and emotionally support our children, providing them with the stability I could not. So, after much thought, prayer, and counsel, I made the decision that what was best for my children was not a choice that society stands by and certainly not my own maternal longing.

Spicuglia—who is working on a book—says, "My hope is that we can take gender out of the expectations around parenting. Half of marriages end in divorce, marriages produce kids and noncustodial parents are a natural byproduct of this process—the fact that this stigma persists is archaic. It's not good for kids, parents, and doesn't reflect the society we're living in."

Indeed it doesn't—parenting and family today look very different from what they looked like thirty years ago. The traditional nuclear family—straight, married, and with biological children gotten the old-fashioned way—is becoming a thing of the past. And it's time for American culture and politics to catch up.

IF YOU WANT HAPPY KIDS, GIVE THEM LESBIAN PARENTS

If you want what's best for your kids, one surefire way to provide them with a healthy, happy home is to make sure they have lesbian parents. In the longest-running study of lesbian families to date,[2] zero percent of children reported physical or sexual abuse—not a one. In the general population, 26 percent of children report physical abuse and 8.3 percent report sexual abuse.

When this news broke, the responses were mixed: It spread like wildfire among LGBT groups and news outlets, the mainstream media reported it as the latest in recent news about LGBT parents being as up to par as straight parents, and—unsurprisingly—conservative groups picked the study apart, trying to find reasons why it was incorrect.

No matter the reactions, however, the study undoubtedly put yet another nail in the coffin of the traditional notion that children need both a mother and a father. This research was just one study in a long line of work showing that children of same-sex parents are just as well adjusted and happy as those raised by heterosexual parents.

A five-year review of eighty-one parenting studies published in the 2010 *Journal of Marriage and Family*,[3] for example, reported that children raised by same-sex parents are "statistically indistinguishable" from those raised by straight parents in terms of self-esteem, academics, and social adjustment. The American Academy of Pediatrics, the Child Welfare League of America, the National Association of Social Workers, the American Medical Association, and the American Psychological Association all agree that same-sex couples are just as fit to parent as their heterosexual counterparts.

Today's "perfect" family is not what it used to be.

In the United States, 29.5 percent of children live in single-parent households (up 10 percent from 1980) and 40.6 percent of children are born to unmarried mothers (up 22 percent since 1980).[4] Most of those unmarried moms are actually in relationships, and a study from Princeton and Columbia, which followed more than five thousand children from birth, found that more than 50 percent of the unmarried parents they studied were living together at the time their baby was born, while 30 percent were in a relationship but not living together.[5]

The use of reproductive technology by straight, gay, married, or unmarried couples is on the rise, and the way Americans choose to create their families is increasingly more fluid. The nuclear family is on the way out.

At the heart of the traditional family there has always been the belief that children need a mother and a father, and that those roles within the family unit are distinct and largely formed around gender difference. The mother is the caretaker, the father the breadwinner and disciplinarian. But today the American public no longer thinks, for the most part, that traditional gender roles and marriages are best.

When the Families and Work Institute ran a survey in 2009, most Americans disagreed with the idea that wives should be the primary caretakers and husbands the primary breadwinners. Other studies, like the one done by sociology professor Lynn Prince Cooke, have shown that straight married couples and parents who forgo traditional gender roles are happier on average then their conventional cohorts. Cooke has noted that, "American couples that share employment and housework are less likely to divorce than couples where the husband does all the earning while the wife does all the cleaning."[6]

Another study found that marriages where husbands do more housework are less likely to end in divorce—so are marriages in which both spouses work. Also in that study, same-sex couples reported sharing domestic responsibilities more equitably than straight couples and having more parental satisfaction.

Interestingly enough, however, even though Americans are more likely to be happy in egalitarian marriage, and don't believe that traditional gender roles within marriage are best, they still believe that when it comes to parenting, marriage is the way to go. In a Pew/*Time* magazine poll on marriage and family,[7] more than 75 percent of respondents said they thought parenting was done best when it's done within a marriage.

But the trend is clear: Straight, nuclear families are no longer the default or the expectation when it comes to having children. That doesn't mean, however, that some people aren't hanging on to traditional roles within families.

The widely held belief that the heterosexual nuclear family is best for children has long been used as a smoke screen for homophobia, and as a talking point to quash marriage-equality efforts. In 2006, the New York Court of Appeals ruled against same-sex marriage because "the Legislature could rationally believe that it is better . . . for children to grow up with both a mother and a father."[8] But, as studies show, it isn't better. Yet that hasn't stopped people from using kids' best interest to make political points.

Studies that purport that straight parents are superior are largely flawed. Instead of comparing straight coupled parents with same-sex coupled parents, these studies contrast straight married couples with straight single mothers and ignore other family-structure variables that have nothing to do with gender.

So why insist on hanging on to an antiquated view based on bad science? Because it's never really been about "the good of the children." In Florida an adoption ban kept kids lingering in foster care while loving gay parents waited in vain; it was overturned only in 2010. And when Washington, D.C., was poised to legalize gay marriage in 2009, the Catholic Archdiocese of Washington ended its foster care program and threatened to stop its social services. (Apparently abandoning children is better than supporting families that don't look like your own.)

There is so much bias around families that aren't created in traditional ways that even access to reproductive technology is under fire. In 2006, for example, a Virginia lawmaker introduced a bill that would forbid unmarried women (single women and lesbians) from using reproductive technology like in vitro fertilization. The bill would have denied unmarried women access to "certain intervening medical technology" that "completely or partially replaces sexual intercourse as the means of conception." And while many states offer insurance coverage for IVF treatments, the person seeking treatment must prove infertility, thereby excluding prospective parents who are LGBT. Some states, like Rhode Island for example, specifically stipulate that insurance will cover the procedures only if a woman's husband provides the sperm. And laws in some states regarding gay and lesbian surrogacy and foster home placement are still ambiguous enough to discriminate.

THE RETURN OF JUNE CLEAVER

The supposed supremacy of the traditional nuclear family isn't just a failing tactic in marriage and family debates; it's a dying convention across the board.

The retrograde belief that children do better in straight families has more to do with gender roles than sexuality. The conservative group Focus on the Family's statement against same-sex marriage, for example, says, "much of the value[9] mothers and fathers bring to their children is due to the fact that female and male are different . . . fathers tend to encourage children to take chances and push limits, and mothers tend to be protective and more cautious." In this way, the push against same-sex marriage is also a push back toward conventional marriage — in every sense of the term.

Families that aren't traditional are viewed, at worst, as damaging or, at best, as "alternative," as if there were a proper default for the makeup of a family.

The pressure is so strong in conservative circles to "protect" traditional family structures that any issue at all can be turned into concern over the nuclear family. When GOP presidential candidates debated one another in Arizona in early 2012, for example, a simple question about support for birth control turned into a debate over babies born out of wedlock. During that debate, CNN moderator John King asked Rick Santorum (who had given an interview about the "dangers" of birth control) about his stance on contraception, and Santorum responded by talking about the American family. "What I was talking about is we have a society . . . which is the increasing number of children being born out of wedlock in America,"[10] he said. "The bottom line is we have a problem in this country, and the family is fracturing. Over 40 percent of children born in America are born out of wedlock. How can a country survive if children are being raised in homes where it's so much harder to succeed economically? . . . No, everything's not going to be fine."

His opponent, Mitt Romney, responded similarly:

This isn't an argument about contraceptives, this is a discussion about, are we going to have a nation which preserves the foundation of the nation, which is the family, or are we not?

When you have 40 percent of kids being born out of wedlock, and among certain ethnic groups the vast majority being born out of wedlock, you ask yourself, How are we going to have a society in the future? We have to have a president who's willing to say that the best opportunity an individual can give to their unborn child is an opportunity to be born in a home with a mother and a father.

But we know already that having a mother and father is *not* the best opportunity we can give a child—having loving parents is. And there's an argument to be made that if intentional and thoughtful parenthood is an indicator of parental and family happiness, then having gay parents—parents who weren't able to "accidentally" have a child—may be, in fact, among the better circumstances there are for a child.

THE NEW NORMAL

We know that the majority of Americans no longer feel that traditional gender roles are necessary, or even desirable. So if we don't support outdated gender norms in our families, why should they have any place in our laws? When Judge Vaughn R. Walker struck down California's Prop 8, for example, he noted that the same-sex marriage ban "exists as an artifact of a time when the genders were seen as having distinct roles in society and in marriage . . . that time has passed."[11]

Traditional roles and families aren't old news for everyone and change isn't going to come easily. But stories like Spicuglia's, which are far from new but only now getting more public attention as "normal" family stories, aren't going away.

This isn't to say that the traditional nuclear family is bad or that it's completely dead—just that it's not necessarily what's best for children. Lesbian-parenting stats aside, no one is really suggesting that all kids would be better off with gay parents than straight ones. But if traditional-family advocates hang on at all costs to their supremacist view of what parenting looks like, it's not just children who will suffer but families and national progress.

There's no one right way to parent and there's no magic combination of genders that produces the most well-adjusted child. We all do the best we can at loving our kids and building our families. So if the goal is happy children, let's focus on that, and not on forcing Americans into an antiquated family model we've moved beyond.

ELEVEN

Women Should Work

The word "choice" has been used, in the context of women
working at home versus working outside the home, as
a euphemism for unpaid labor, with no job security, no
health or vacation benefits and no retirement plan. No
wonder men are not clamoring for this "choice."

— *Barbara Cohn Schlachet, Letter to the
Editor, The New York Times, 2006*

I N 2010, *The Washington Post* published an article about
whether or not moms who work outside of the home have
a negative impact on their child's well-being. It ran under
the headline, "Working Mothers Not Necessarily Harmful to
Child Development."[1] Despite the painfully lukewarm title,
working mothers and feminists rejoiced.

The article cited a study out of Columbia University based
on the largest child care study ever done, in which more than
one thousand children were followed by the National Institute of Child Health and Human Development of Early
Child Care. The Columbia study marked the first time that

researchers measured the full effect of working moms on their
children: not just the ways in which maternal employment
could hurt children, but the positive effects that it could have
on kids as well. The study's takeaway was that, "the overall effect of 1st year maternal employment on child development is neutral." While a conclusion of "neutral" doesn't
seem particularly revelatory or celebration-worthy for working mothers—who have been hearing for decades about the
various ways in which they are irrevocably damaging their
children—it was an indisputable win.

There was the study that told working mothers that they
would force their daughters into early puberty,[2] for example,
not only tapping into the omnipresent guilt so many working
mothers face but hitting on fears around the increased sexu-
alization of young girls in American culture. Or the 2010 research from the University of Chicago purporting that working mothers had children with higher BMIs (body mass
indexes) than mothers who stayed at home. The media ran
with that study with headlines like, "The More Mom Works,
the Heavier Her Kids Get"[3] and "Mom's Work Schedule Is
Making Kids Fat."[4] One study from North Carolina State
University even reported that working mothers had negative
impacts on their children's health—that women who worked
were more likely to have sick children.[5] "Stay-at-home moms
may have been right all along when their maternal instincts
told them they are the best equipped to care for their children," one newspaper scolded.

Caryl Rivers points out in *Selling Anxiety: How the
News Media Scare Women* that public and cultural backlash
against women becoming more active in the public sphere is
hardly new. She writes, "When women were pressing for the
vote, the media of the era were fairly hysterical on the sub-

ject. It was said that if women left home to enter the polling booth, they would cease to be the angels of the hearth that men so admired, would become coarse and crass and thus incapable of being good mothers, and the family would be destroyed."

Sound familiar? The media narrative around women working—particular *mothers* working—tells a story that goes beyond headlines. It marks American cultural progress and demonstrates the way in which the myths of parenthood are created, the realities ignored, and the way they're both consumed by a public desperate for answers and validation.

The truth about parenting and working is much more nuanced than a well-placed headline, and the reality of mothers—whether they work or stay at home—is more complex than any one "right" answer. Just because it's complicated, however, doesn't mean that there isn't a clear truth. There is an undeniable reality of women's lives and tangible ways in which their decisions around work and family affect their lives, their children's lives, and even society at large.

OPTING IN, OPTING OUT, LET'S CALL THE WHOLE THING OFF

When Lisa Belkin wrote an article in *The New York Times Magazine* in 2003[6] about motherhood, she asked a question—and provided an answer—that would both enrapture and infuriate American women: "Why don't women run the world? Maybe it's because they don't want to."

Belkin's cover story profiled a handful of elite mothers—Ivy league–educated women who worked at banks or law firms, had MBAs and husbands with large salaries—who were "rejecting the workplace."

As these women look up at the "top," they are increasingly deciding that they don't want to do what it takes to get there. Women today have the equal right to make the same bargain that men have made for centuries—to take time from their family in pursuit of success. Instead, women are redefining success. And in doing so, they are redefining work.

Time was when a woman's definition of success was said to be her apple-pie recipe. Or her husband's promotion. Or her well-turned-out children. Next, being successful required becoming a man. Remember those awful padded-shoulder suits and floppy ties? Success was about the male definition of money and power.

There is nothing wrong with money or power. But they come at a high price. And lately when women talk about success they use words like satisfaction, balance and sanity.

Vicky McElhaney Benedict, for example, went to Princeton University and then on to Duke University School of Law. When Belkin interviewed her, she had two children and was a stay-at-home mom. "This is what I was meant to do," she said. "I hate to say that because it sounds like I could have skipped college. But I mean this is what I was meant to do at this time. I know that's very un-p.c., but I like life's rhythms when I'm nurturing a child."

The article was outrageously popular—it was the top emailed story on the site and it seemed as if anyone who had ever written anything about motherhood or women was talking or writing about it. Most of the criticism of Belkin's piece (including my own, at the time) focused on the fact that she chose to pin a trend on such a small, elite subset of women. What did it matter if a tiny percentage of rich women were staying at home? That didn't seem to mean much in terms of big-picture concerns of American mothers, most of whom couldn't forgo an income even if they wanted to.

Belkin was careful to note the limits of her thesis in the article, writing that she realized this was "true mostly of elite, successful women who can afford real choice—who have partners with substantial salaries and health insurance—making it easy to dismiss them as exceptions." But, she argued, "these are the very women who were supposed to be the professional equals of men right now, so the fact that so many are choosing otherwise is explosive."

Linda Hirshman, lawyer and feminist author of the controversial book manifesto *Get to Work*, thinks the critique that women like those in Belkin's article are statistically insignificant is beside the point. "Social change often comes top down," she told me. "The fact that most women can't afford to make this decision doesn't change the social resonance of it—it's the regime effect."

Hirshman says that mothers like the ones Belkin interviewed aren't making decisions in a social vacuum and that their choice has a profound social and political effect on other women. If staying at home becomes the desired choice as demonstrated by the upper echelon of parents, Hirshman believes, then that is going to impact the way that *all* women look at mothering.

Other critics focused their ire on the message that these women were sending by staying home instead of being out in the workplace. Katie Allison Granju, now the popular blogger behind Mamapundit, wrote[7] that Belkin's piece didn't consider the consequences for women—even if they are of an elite class—who make the decision to stay at home. "Like Belkin, I too smugly pontificated about the many joys and benefits of creating a work life that allowed me to nurture my family and explore my own creativity. I patted myself on the back for my willingness to forego a full-time, salaried job in my field to be a better mother," Granju wrote at a website for mothers.

But, she explained, that kind of comfy existence doesn't necessarily last forever. Granju wrote about her divorce, and the shock of suddenly becoming a single mother to three children,

> no longer living in a house I own, and cobbling together a living without the benefit of a live-in spousal income. But is this a surprise? Didn't women my age learn the risks of depending too heavily on our spouses for future economic security by watching middle-aged women who had been full-time mothers limp into the workforce in droves as divorce rates skyrocketed during the 70s and 80s? These women—many of whom had cultivated careers or at least career skills in the years before marriage and motherhood—found that their voluntary sabbatical from the labor force left them ill-equipped to support themselves, much less pay for health care or save for retirement.

Granju's complaint was prescient; eight years after Belkin's piece was published, writer Katy Read wrote, "Regrets of a Stay-at-Home Mom" for Salon.[8] The subhead read, "Consider this a warning to new mothers: Fourteen years ago, I 'opted out' to focus on my family. Now I'm broke." Read wrote that she wasn't worried about the financial consequences of staying at home with her kids in part because "nobody else seemed to be."

> Most articles and books about what came to be called "opting out" focused on the budgeting challenges of dropping to one paycheck—belt-tightening measures shared by both par-

ents—while barely touching on the longer-term sacrifices borne primarily by the parent who quits: the lost promotions, raises and retirement benefits; the atrophied skills and frayed professional networks. The difficulty of reentering the workforce after years away was underreported, the ramifications of divorce, widowhood or a partner's layoff hardly considered. It was as though at-home mothers could count on being financially supported happily ever after, as though a permanent and fully employed spouse were the new Prince Charming.

It isn't just divorce that puts women who have "opted out" into the position of having to earn an income again. In 2009, *The New York Times*[9] ran a story in their business section about women who had been staying at home being forced back into the labor market because the recession took their husbands' jobs. The economic reality of not having an income—and not building professional skills and contacts—cannot be ignored.

Controversy and criticism aside, articles like Belkin's have framed the debate around working mothers since their publication, so even if you take issue with their content, they're central to the cultural understanding of work/life balance in the United States.

Two years after Belkin's "opt out revolution" piece was published, for example, the *Times* ran a similar article, "Many Women at Elite Colleges Set Career Path to Motherhood."[10] It ran on the front page of the paper and claimed that 60 percent of female Yale students interviewed indicated that they would cut back on work or stop working entirely once they had children.

Like Belkin's article, this one—written by Louise Story— was also widely read and widely criticized. Bloggers, feminists, and even other reporters took issue with the story not only because of its narrow focus—again, why a trend piece about such a small percentage of the population?—but also because of what was seen as shoddy reporting. Jack Shafer of Slate,[11] for example, counted the number of "weasel words" like *some* and *many* that were used in place of statistics and data.

To Linda Hirshman—again, who believes the regime effect is just as important as statistics—the social impact of elite stay-at-home mothers is a central part of feminism, and parenting. "Setting aside for a moment the people who have to work," she told me, "an important question is why do they do it? It's like the really skinny models; it's some bizarre norm of female accomplishment that no one can really achieve."

Hirshman argues that women who choose to stay at home and raise children—especially those who are of the privileged upper-middle-class variety—are doing a disservice to other women and society at large. In *Get to Work* she writes that women who don't work outside the home aren't fully using their intellectual capacities: "Whether they leave the workplace altogether or just cut back their commitment, their talent and education is lost from the public world to the private world of laundry and kissing boo-boos. The abandonment of the public world by women at the top means the ruling class is overwhelmingly male. If the rulers are male, they will make mistakes that benefit males."

Hirshman also asked a question that doesn't come up as often as it used to: If more and more women become stay-at-home moms, what will that mean for the women of America? It seems to be a question that no one is very comfortable answering, in part—once more—because of the increase of American individualism and the move away from community. Vicky McElhaney Benedict, one of the women Belkin interviewed, for example, said: "I've had people tell me that it's women like me that are ruining the workplace because it makes employers suspicious. I don't want to take on the mantle of all womanhood and fight a fight for some sister who isn't really my sister because I don't even know her." We're all in it for ourselves!

The other reason that Hirshman's question raises hackles is that feminism has increasingly come to be understood as a movement that gives women access to more choices, so if you want to stay at home, stay at home. If it's your choice, it's the right one.

But Hirshman sees the rise of "choice feminism" as a huge step backward for women. "A woman who decides staying home with her children matters more than the fate of other women ought to be prepared to defend that position," she writes. "The position that women's choices are unworthy of moral analysis raises the ugly possibility that women's choices don't matter because women don't matter."

HAPPY HOMEMAKERS?

If American mothers aren't comfortable with the moral question about how their work decisions affect society more broadly, they should at the very least be concerned how those choices affect themselves and their own happiness. Are stay-at-home mothers happier and more fulfilled than their working counterparts? Is there any easy answer?

What we do know for sure is that the media has long hyped articles that show working mothers are miserable — that they've somehow compromised their own happiness and their children's well-being. An MSNBC headline read, "Working Moms Trying to Do It All May Be More Depressed."[12] *Working Mother* magazine promises "10 Secrets to Being Happy,"[13] and CBS asked, "Why Are Women so Unhappy at Work?"[14] Many of these pieces target feminism and women's advancement as the source of how female happiness has soured. Maureen Dowd complained that the more women have achieved, "the more they seem aggrieved."[15] As the title of Ross Douthat's *New York Times* piece put it, we're supposedly "Liberated and Unhappy."[16]

But does this cultural certainty match reality?

Caryl Rivers in *Selling Anxiety* says no: "You would think that something—or someone—was forcing all these miserable women to stay at their jobs, instead of running home where they would really be happy. But what does reliable social science say? . . . Nearly two decades of well-designed, reliable research find working women consistently healthy—healthier, in fact, than homemakers."

She points to several national studies showing that women who work had better physical and emotional health than their stay-at-home counterparts. One twenty-two-year-long study out of UC Berkeley showed that by the time stay-at-home mothers turned forty-three, they had more chronic health conditions and were more frustrated and jaded than women with jobs outside the home. Another major study found that it wasn't having a baby that increased emotional unhappiness for women; it was having a baby *and* quitting your job.

Rivers's stats hold up today as well. A 2011 study from the American Psychological Association showed that mothers who had jobs during their children's infancy and preschool years were more likely to be happy and healthy than women who stayed at home.[17] Mothers who worked had better health and fewer depression symptoms.

Researcher Cheryl Buehler, a professor of human development and family studies at the University of North Carolina in Greensboro, noted that what made mothers happiest and increased their general well-being was working part time, over working full time or staying at home. "However, in many cases the well-being of moms working part time was no different from moms working full time," she said.[18]

It's easy to argue that women who have rewarding careers shouldn't quit them, of course. Or that society needs more women lawyers, doctors, judges, and CEOs. But a lot of American mothers who leave their jobs aren't necessarily leaving behind fulfilling employment. For every pro-work feminist complaint that stay-at-home motherhood is a thankless job chock-full of repetitive tasks and lacking in intellectual stimulation, there's a woman who will show you that her job is exactly that—minus the time with her kids.

For those women who have soul crushingly boring jobs, the "choice" to stay at home can be a bit more clear-cut. But when it comes to moms whose jobs are indisputably mind numbing, American culture doesn't really care if they stay at home. In fact, when women in low-paying professions or working-class mothers *don't* work, they're likely to be called lazy rather than venerated as concerned and involved mothers.

Women who receive government assistance, for example, aren't told by the media (or anyone else) to stay home and take care of their kids. Even though their child care benefits are paltry and jobs scarce and underpaying, no one suggests that low-income women should be stay-at-home moms. Interestingly enough, however, there are marriage-incentive programs for women on welfare, which means that they have financial incentives to become or stay married. Yet another way to push traditional gender roles onto women and mothers (men on welfare have no such incentives).

For most mothers, working is a given—the majority of American families need dual incomes to survive. The way in which we talk about who is a good mother and who should be a stay-at-home mother, however, reveals that the cultural perceptions around work/life balance have less to do with economics and reality and more to do with embracing a myth of parenthood that pits women with children against each other.

THE NUMBERS

Caryl Rivers says that the "real story about young women is that females at elite colleges want good jobs with reasonable hours, so that they can have adequate time with their families." I imagine that's not just the hope of women at elite colleges—but most American women. Rivers writes that nuanced stories about women's work and motherhood wants don't get a lot of "buzz," and they "certainly would not [appear] on the front page of the *Times*."

Joan Williams, a law professor and director at the Center for WorkLife Law, did a study " 'Opt Out' or Pushed Out?: How the Press Covers Work/Family Conflict," in 2006 of the way that mainstream media covers work/family issues. In particular, Williams looked at whether women pulled out of work, or were pushed out, and the way in which the press misconstrued those two circumstances.

In her report, Williams found that almost 75 percent of the stories analyzed focused on the "pull" rather than the "push."[19] In fact, there were very few mentions of the way that mothers are pushed out of workforce. That didn't jibe with the reality; Williams points to a 2004 study that showed 86 percent of women surveyed said they quit for work-related reasons such as workplace inflexibility, not because they wanted to. Only 6 percent of the stories Williams and her colleagues analyzed identified women being pushed out of work as to why they were staying at home. The report also found that most media coverage reported on work/life issues as if they were something only professional women or women in high-status jobs experienced. This is not the case.

The truth of the numbers is much different. *The Washington Post* revisited the "opt-out revolution" in 2009,[20] arguing that new census numbers proved that there was no such revolution happening. Staff writer Donna St. George wrote that 2009 census information—which was collected as a direct response to the opt-out media mania—showed that stay-at-home mothers were not the elite upper class that Belkin focused on, but instead were younger, less educated, and had lower incomes. Almost one in five stay-at-home mothers had less than a high school degree (it was one in twelve for other mothers), and only 32 percent had an undergraduate degree. Of the stay-at-home mothers, 12 percent were living below the poverty line, compared to 5 percent of other moms.

Diana Elliott, a coauthor of the census report and a family demographer, told the *Post*, "I do think there is a small population, a very small population, that is opting out, but with the nationally representative data, we're just not seeing that."

What they did see, however, was that stay-at-home moms were not limited to one subset of women. Almost one in four married mothers—5.6 million women—stay at home with their kids. (Only 165,000 fathers do the same.) They also found that despite the public face of stay-at-home momism being overwhelmingly white, 27 percent of stay-at-home mothers were Hispanic and 34 percent were born outside of the United States.

But who is staying at home and who is working doesn't answer the question of *why*— or *if* we should be asking that question at all.

I CHOOSE MY CHOICE

When Hirshman's book was first published, like many feminists I was quick to criticize it. I thought *Get to Work*'s tone was harsh and judgmental. Who was she—who was anyone—to tell women what the "right" choice was for their family? I was tired of the articles claiming one kind of parenthood was better than another, and rolled my eyes whenever I saw a fight break out on a blog or forum about whether working moms or stay-at-home moms were doing the best for their kids. But the truth is, while I was uncomfortable with the idea of mandating—or even suggesting—to women that there's one better choice, I actually believe that there is.

We need flexible work schedules, paid maternity leave (that lasts more than a few weeks or months), subsidized child care, and workplaces that are parent friendly. I also worry about the financial security of women who don't have paying jobs. I don't think it's a good idea to depend on someone else financially for an extended period of time. In a perfect world, the United States would provide a wage for housework and child care—after all, it's labor that contributes to the economy, whether it's formally recognized or not. But that's not the world we live in right now. I'm not sure how to reconcile these beliefs with my feeling that people's life choices should

be honored. I think there's a way to discuss and think critically—and be critical—of parents' choices without resorting
to personal attacks and hyperbole. And I trust women and
mothers to be able to have this conversation with the knowledge that we want to make parents' lives better.

TWELVE

Why Have Kids?

Children have never been very good at listening to their elders, but they have never failed to imitate them.

— *James Baldwin*

M EGAN SAYS SHE fell into a traditional mothering role "by default."

"I'm in charge of stories, bathing, and picking out outfits. I order everything in the house, making sure toys are in the place and that the dogs aren't eating the crayons. If I died tomorrow, I don't think my kids' nails would ever be cut again."

Megan, who is from Mount Laurel, New Jersey, says she feels like she's turned into her mother, making stereotypical proclamations to her kids that she swore she never would—like threatening to throw her children's toys away if they aren't cleaned up (with a trash bag in hand for full effect).

Her children are five and three years old now, but she says being a new mother was the worst of it. After Megan had her first child, she and a friend in her "little yuppie townhouse development" who also had a new child would walk together every night with the babies in strollers. Sometimes, she says, with a small glass of wine in the stroller's cup holder. One night, Megan says, her friend looked over at her and said, "I know this sounds terrible, but I understand why there are moms out there that shake their babies." Megan agreed.

"Does that make me a terrible person?" she asks.

Megan says she never could have imagined how her life would change once she had children. "They don't come with instructions, they change every week, you can't figure them out . . . they defy logic. Suddenly getting to go to the grocery store by yourself is like a five-star vacation," she told me. "Even your purse is gone and you have this ten-pound diaper bag. Your clothes are covered in baby barf, but why bother getting dressed at all—nothing fits anyway."

Megan says she was able to get over her post-baby blues, and went back to work eight weeks after her son was born. But still, she says, she was spread too thin. Work felt like a vacation from her parenting responsibilities, but she was still incredibly stressed and felt like she wasn't doing anything well—at work or at home.

Two years later she had a daughter. Now, Megan says, "things aren't perfect and I try not to expect them to be."

"Kids whine, they cry; they ruin movies and vacations. I once had to get off a train because my kid was crying so hard. I've exchanged words with an old lady at church who told me my kid needed to stop whispering and was rude. I've lost my temper in public. I've had to buy groceries that had pee on them when my kid peed in the cart."

Megan says being raised to believe that women can do it all "bit her in the ass." "We can't," she told me, "and that's okay. I can't cook, do laundry, check homework, do my own job, grade my students' essays, take care of the dogs, and get my stuff ironed. I do the best I can. And if I have dirty floors, that's okay. I'd rather have my sanity."

Perhaps Megan has figured out the answer to parental happiness—at least on a personal level. She doesn't do it all. She doesn't expect perfection from herself or her kids. She *embraces* the frazzle.

Of course, that's easy to do when you're financially comfortable and don't have to worry about big-picture issues surrounding your child. But still, she's onto something.

THE AGE OF ANXIETY

Peter Stearns, author of *Anxious Parents: A History of Modern Childrearing in America,* argues that parental anxiety and worry are a relatively new phenomenon. In the 1930s, for example, studies showed that marriages with and without children were equally happy. By the 1950s, however, marriages with no children became significantly happier than their child-laden counterparts. Stearns also reports that even among people who are already parents, the happiest among them are those who spend the least time with their kids—divorced dads. "Consistently, the less time spent with one's children, the more positive one's parenting experience," he writes. Perhaps even more disturbing to hands-on parents, "the more active the parents, the more they report feelings of inadequacy, negativity, and ambivalence."

It makes sense, then, that five times as many parenting-advice books were published in 1997 as were in 1975—an industry built itself around a nation of parental worriers.

Stearns argues that the twentieth century marked the first

time that childhood was seen as something separate and distinct from adulthood, rather than just a prelude to becoming an adult. He writes, "Contemporary children were seen as more fragile, readily overburdened, requiring careful handling or even outright favoritism lest their shaky self-esteem be crushed. Notions of children's fragility obviously caused new levels of parental anxiety, but they were also a reflection of these anxieties."

And as worries about children's health declined, anxiety about everything else spiked: schooling, chores around the house, how they should spend leisure time.

With this shift, American parents started to set high standards from what they expected from children—and from parenthood. "Behind many worries has lurked the guilty suspicion that having children was not as satisfactory as had been expected, a thought whose subversiveness could heighten anxiety in its own right," Stearns writes.

With increased expectations came increased unhappiness—and anxiety. Sounds familiar? For every detail that parents obsess and fret over, they are increasing their level of stress, unhappiness, and dissatisfaction. And for what?

When I met with Linda Hirshman to talk about her work, she told a story of injuring her hand. She plays the piano, so she did a ton of physical therapy to regain as much use of her hand as possible. She found, however, that she had lost a full key of reach—so back to hand therapy she went. But her therapist told her that if she were to spend another year in physical therapy, she would add maybe 1 percent of functionality back to her playing. She related this story to the incredible amount of work and anxiety parents, mothers in particular, put into their children. "If you're giving 80 percent of your life to your children, maybe you'll add 1 percent of difference in your child's life," she says. Assuming you're in a position in which you don't have to worry about the basic needs, and can provide your child a good life, how much extra work will really make *that* much of a difference?

GIVING UP CONTROL

I was not well prepared for parenthood—at least, not the way it happened to me.

While Layla was in the hospital, I scrubbed the nursery floors, bought a top-of-the-line air purifier, and folded onesies (the small shape of which, I have to tell you, don't really lend themselves to folding) with an OCD-like glint in my eye. Not because I thought my daughter actually needed a particularly neat room or well-organized clothes but because there wasn't anything else I could do for her. She was connected to wires and breathing machines and I couldn't hold her for more than a couple of minutes at a time. The medical uncertainty, Layla's suffering, and the pain her prematurity caused my whole family was completely out of my control. So I cleaned.

My case is an extreme example, to be sure, but the feeling that drove me is one I believe most parents can relate to. When we parent, we're trying desperately to control an inherently uncontrollable situation.

We don't have control over whether or not our babies will be ill or disabled, premature or otherwise hurt. Most of us have no say over whether the child care available to us will be affordable, if our job will offer maternity leave, or if our boss will let us leave early to pick up our sick kid from school.

We can't stop bad things from happening—our children from being bullied, our neighborhoods from being unsafe, or the world from being unfair.

So parents focus on the things they can control. For some, that means buying expensive strollers and over-scheduling their kid with French tutors and piano lessons. For others, it's simply making sure their kid is well fed and put together as they leave the house. No matter what the worry is, however, it's always there. I'm sure some parents have learned to let go, but I haven't met many of them.

The truth about parenting is that the reality of our lives needs to be enough. Seeking out an ideal that most of us can never reach is making us, and our kids, miserable. There are certain things we *do* have control over, that we can use to change parenting in America.

First and foremost, we need to start thinking about raising our children as a community exercise. Shifting our consciousness in this way has the potential to change so much. When we take the pressure off ourselves to be the one and only caregiver for our children, it will not only free us from the increasing loneliness of solitary caretaking but also open a world of love and support to our children. When we think about society, instead of just our individual kids, it makes it that much easier to demand government and workplace policies that honor parenting for everyone. We can fight for extended paid leave for all parents.

We need to do away with the idea that there is a "natural" way to parent—whatever way we choose to parent *is* the natural way. Once we let go of a maternal (and paternal) ideal that doesn't exist, we can do the real work of loving our kids and have fun doing it.

American parents need to support one another—especially those of us who don't fit into the "good" or "perfect" mother model. When one mother is punished, we're all punished. We can fight against policies that criminalize mothers for being mothers and that dictate that women are less than human when they're pregnant. We also need to accept that the world is changing, and that there isn't one kind of family, so we need to support all kinds, not just in our personal lives but in our political and social actions.

Megan says that for as many imperfect moments there are while mothering, the highs make it all worth it. "Snuggling, hearing 'Mommy, I love you the most,' fixing boo-boos."

I agree. But focusing on the happy moments can take us only so far. We deserve more than just moments of parental joy. We deserve, and can get, a life of them.

Acknowledgments

I owe a huge debt of gratitude to my editor, Julia Cheiffetz, who helped conceive of the idea for this book and has had nothing but faith in me from the moment we met. Anything that is good in this book is thanks to her. Her patience and kind but firm editing made this book what it is. Thanks also go to Carly Hoffmann and the rest of the incredible team at Amazon.

Thanks to my agent, Tracy Brown, who is a wonderful advisor and friend and who always has my back. I also owe tremendous gratitude to my good friend Gwendolyn Beetham, who was gracious enough to lend me her incredible research and synthesizing skills when I needed them most.

Heartfelt thanks to my family—Andrew especially—for encouraging me to continue writing even when it felt impossible to do so.

Most importantly, thank you to the parents who shared their stories with me for this book. Your honesty and openness was refreshing, terrifying, and fascinating; you made writing this book a joy.

Notes

INTRODUCTION

1 "No one has nannies—so can we please stop writing about them?" Sara Mosle. *Slate.* February 4, 2010.
2 "Breastfeeding Data and Statistics." Centers for Disease Control and Prevention. August 2, 2011. http://www.cdc.gov/breastfeeding/data/
3 "For Women Who Want Kids, 'the Sooner the Better': 90 Percent of Eggs Gone By Age 30." Roger Fortuna. *Good Morning America.* January 29, 2010.
4 "Early Puberty for Girls of Working Moms." Madeline Holler. Babble.com. September 3, 2010.
5 "Do Preschools and Nannies Turn Kids Into Bullies?" Jessica Reaves. *Time.* April 19, 2001.
6 "Declines in Marital Satisfaction Among New Mothers: Broad Strokes Versus Fine Details." Mari L. Clements, Sarah E. Martin, Amanda K. Cassil, Niveen N. Soliman. *Journal of Marriage and Family.* February 2011.
7 "Mother Madness." Erica Jong. *Wall Street Journal.* November 6, 2010.
8 "All the Single Ladies." Kate Bolick. *Atlantic.* November 2011.

1. CHILDREN MAKE YOU HAPPY

1 "Forever Pregnant." January Payne. *The Washington Post.* May 16, 2006.
2 "Recommendations to Improve Preconception Health and Care." Centers for Disease Control and Prevention. April 21, 2006. http://www.cdc.gov/mmwr/preview/mmwrhtml/rr5506a1.htm
3 "Preconception Screening and Counseling Checklist." March of Dimes.

4 "Study O.K.'s Light Drinking During Pregnancy. Too Good to Be True?" *Time.* October 6, 2010.

5 "Study Shows 1 in 10 Dads Has Moderate to Severe Postpartum Depression." Charlene Laino. *WebMD Health News.*

6 "More Than Half of Poor Infants Have Mothers Showing Signs of Depression." The Urban Institute. August 26, 2010.

7 "PBS Tackles Happiness In 'This Emotional Life'." NPR. January 4, 2010.

2. WOMEN ARE THE NATURAL PARENT

1 "Being There: Attached Parents." Tara Brown. *60 Minutes* (Australia). October 22, 2006.

2 "Home Births Grow More Popular in the U.S." NPR. January 26, 2012.

3 "The Impossibility of "Natural Parenting for Modern Mothers." Petra Buskens. *Journal of the Association for Research on Mothering.* Spring/Summer 2001.

4 Blue Milk blog. http://bluemilk.wordpress.com/

5 Jong, Erica. "Mother Madness" *Wall Street Journal.* November 6, 2010.

6 Granju, Katie Allison, and Jillian St. Charles."Has Attachment Parenting Imprisoned Mothers?" *New York Times.* November 10, 2010.

7 Jong-Fast, Molly. "Growing Up with Ma Jong." *Wall Street Journal.* November 6, 2010.

4. CHILDREN NEED THEIR PARENTS

1 "The Census Bureau Counts Fathers as 'Child Care'." KJ Dell'Antonia. *The New York Times,* February 8, 2012.

2 "Who's Minding the Kids? Child Care Arrangements." U.S. Census Bureau. August 2010. http://www.census.gov/prod/2010pubs/p70-121.pdf

3 "The Republican Mother: Women and the Enlightenment." Linda Kerber, *American Quarterly.* Summer 1976.

4 Toossi, Mitra. "A century of change: The U.S. labor force, 1950–2050." Bureau of Labor Statistics. May 2002.

5 Belsky, Jay. "The 'Effects' of Infant Day Care Reconsidered." ERIC Clearinghouse on Elementary and Early Childhood Education. 1987.

6 Talbot, Margaret. "The Devil in the Nursery." *New York Times.* January 7, 2001.

7 Flanagan, Caitlin. "How Serfdom Saved the Women's Movement." *Atlantic.* March 2004.

8 "Who's the Fairest Wife of Them All?" Laurie Abraham. *ELLE.* March 16, 2006.

9 "Paradise Lost (Domestic Division)." Terry Martin Hekker. *New York Times.* January 1, 2006.

10 "Times are Changing: Gender and Generation at Work and at Home." Ellen

Galinsky. Families and Work Institute. August 2011. http://familiesandwork
.org/site/research/reports/Times_Are_Changing.pdf
11 "The New Dad: Caring, Committed and Conflicted." Brad Harrington, Boston
College. 2011.
12 "Even in Academia, Dads Don't Do Diapers." Cristina Lindblad. *Business Week.*
February 21, 2012.
13 "America's Children: Key National Indicators of Well-Being, 2011." Federal In-
teragency Forum on Child and Family Statistics. 2011. http://www.childstats
.gov/americaschildren/
14 "Cuts to Child Care Subsidy Thwart More Job Seekers." Peter Goodman. *New
York Times.* May 23, 2010.
15 "Parents and the High Cost of Child Care: 2010 Update." National Association
of Child Care Resource and Referral Agencies. 2010.
16 "The Care Crisis." Ruth Rosen. *The Nation.* March 12, 2007.

5. "THE HARDEST JOB IN THE WORLD"

1 "The Hardest Job in the World?" Megan Francis. *Babble.* September 21, 2009.
2 "Kristi," "Is Motherhood the Hardest Job in the World?" Interrupted Wander-
lust. September 29, 2009.
3 Anonymous. "Hardest Job in the World?" My Ruminations. September 23,
2009.
4 Kung, Michelle. "The Mommy Wars: Dr. Laura on Stay-at-Home Moms." *Wall
Street Journal.* April 8, 2009.
5 Brooks, David. "The Year of Domesticity." *New York Times.* January 1, 2006.
6 Traister, Rebecca. "At Home with David Brooks." Salon.com. January 4, 2006.

6. MOTHER KNOWS BEST

1 http://skepchick.org/

7. GIVING UP ON PARENTHOOD

1 Governor Dave Heinemen. "Change Made to Safe Haven Law." November 24,
2008.
2 "Hate Being a Mom." http://www.secret-confessions.com/hate/hate-being-a
-mom
3 "Facts on Publicly Funded Contraceptive Services in the United States." Guttmacher Institute. May 2012.
4 Barber, Jennifer. "Home and Parenting Resources Available to Siblings Depending on Their Birth Intention Status." *Child Development.* May/June 2009.

5   "America's Child Death Shame." BBC News. October 17, 2011. http://www.bbc
    .co.uk/news/world-us-canada-15288865
6   "Child Maltreatment 2010." Administration for Children and Families. http://
    www.acf.hhs.gov/programs/cb/pubs/cm10/index.htm
7   "Custodial Mothers and Fathers and Their Child Support: 2009." U.S. Census
    Bureau.
8   "Ads Urge Fathers to 'Take Time' to Be a Dad." *New York Times.* October 18,
    2010.
9   Fairyington, Stephanie. "The Parent Trap: Paternal Rights and Abortion." *ELLE*
    magazine. May 17, 2010.
10 Cailard, Cynthia. "The Drive to Enact 'Infant Abandonment' Laws — A Rush to
    Judgment?" The Guttmacher Report on Public Policy. August 2000.

8. "BAD" MOTHERS GO TO JAIL

1   "Pregnant and Dangerous." Katha Pollitt. *The Nation.* April 8, 2004.
2   "Utah Continues Reckless Efforts to Lock Up Pregnant Women." Lynn Paltrow.
    The Huffington Post. March 6, 2010.
3   Horowitz, Emily. "Murder by Nursing?" *RH Reality Check.* February 21, 2012.
4   Horowitz, Emily. "Murder by Nursing?" *RH Reality Check.* February 21, 2012.
5   "Theft Charge Dismissed Against Ohio Mom Kelley Williams-Bolar." Jamilah
    King. *Colorlines.* February 1, 2011.
6   Hing, Julianne. "Tanya McDowell Pleads Not Guilty to 'Stealing' Son's Educa-
    tion," *Colorlines.* April 27, 2011.
7   Peveteaux, April. "Pregnant Mom Sacrifices Life So Baby Can Live." CafeMom.
    October 17, 2011.
8   "The Martyrdom of Jenni Lake." Daily Kos. http://www.dailykos.com/story
    /2011/12/29/1049743/--I-did-what-I-was-supposed-to-do-The-Martyrdom-of
    -Jenni-Lake

9. SMART WOMEN DON'T HAVE KIDS

1   Marcotte, Amanda. "The Real Reason More Women Are Childless." *Slate.* July
    12, 2010.
2   "Childlessness Up Among All Women; Down Among Women with Advanced
    Degrees." Gretchen Livingston and D'Vera Cohn. Pew Research Center. June
    25, 2010.
3   "Having Kids Makes You Happy." *Newsweek.* June 28, 2008.
4   "Childlessness Bothers Men More Than Women." Carolyn Colwell. HealthDay.
5   "Feminism's Uneven Success." Nancy Folbre. *New York Times.* December 19,
    2011.

6 "Dynamics of the Gender Gap for Young Professionals in the Financial and Corporate Sectors." Marianne Bertrand, Claudia Goldin, and Lawrence F. Katz. *American Economic Journal: Applied Economics.* July 2010.

7 "Gender at Core." Catalyzing, August 5, 2010. http://www.catalyst.org/blog /gender-stereotypes/gender-at-core

8 "I Cannot Truly Want What I Am Told I Must Have." Melissa McEwan, *Shakesville.* February 22, 2012. http://www.shakesville.com/2012/02/icannot-truly-want -what-i-am-told-i.html

9 Lisa Hymas. "Say it loud—I'm childfree and I'm proud." The Grist. March 31, 2010.

10. DEATH OF THE NUCLEAR FAMILY

1 "What Kind of Mother Leaves Her Kids?" Lea Goldman. *Marie Claire.* July 8, 2009.

2 Gartrell, Nanette, Henny M. W. Bos, and Naomi G. Goldberg. "Adolescents of the U.S. National Longitudinal Lesbian Family Study: Sexual Orientation, Sexual Behavior, and Sexual Risk Exposure." National Longitudinal Lesbian Family Study. June 2010.

3 Biblarz, Timothy, and Judith Stacey. "Does the Gender of Parents Matter?" *Journal of Marriage and Family.* February 2010.

4 "Statistical Abstract of the United States." U.S. Census Bureau. 2012.

5 "Who Needs Marriage? A Changing Institution." Belinda Luscombe. *TIME.* November 18, 2010.

6 "'Traditional' Marriages Now Less Stable Than Ones Where Couples Share Work and Household Chores." Lynn Price Cooke. Council on Contemporary Families. July 5, 2008.

7 "Who Needs Marriage? A Changing Institution." Belinda Luscombe. *TIME.* November 18, 2010.

8 Biskupic, Joan. "Same-sex marriage fails at NY Court." *USA Today.* July 7, 2006.

9 Tyree, Jenny. "Mom and Dad: Kids Need Both." Focus on the Family. June 15, 2010.

10 Full Transcript of CNN Arizona Republican Presidential Debate. February 22, 2012.

11 Editorial. "Marriage Is a Constitutional Right." *New York Times.* August 4, 2010.

11. WOMEN SHOULD WORK

1 "Study: Working Mothers Not Necessarily Harmful to Child Development." Daniel de Vise. *The Washington Post.* July 31, 2010.

2   "Early Disconnect with Mom May Speed Onset of Puberty in Girls." Melissa Healy. *The Los Angeles Times.* September 1, 2010.

3   "The More Mom Works, the Heavier Her Kids Get: Study." Madonna Behen. *Business Week,* February 4, 2011.

4   "Study: Moms' Work Schedule Is Making Kids Fat." *Fox News.* February 4, 2011.

5   "Report: Moms with Jobs Have Sicker Kids." *McClatchy Newspapers.* February 18, 2011.

6   "The Opt-Out Revolution." Lisa Belkin. *New York Times.* October 26, 2003.

7   "The Case Against 'Opting-Out.'" Katie Allison Granju. *The Mother's Movement Online.* January 2004.

8   "Regrets of a Stay-at-home Mom." Katy Read. *Salon.com.* January 5, 2011.

9   "Recession Drives Women Back to the Work Force." Steven Greenhouse. *New York Times.* September 18, 2009.

10 Story, Louise. "Many Women at Elite Colleges Set Career Path to Motherhood." *New York Times.* September 20, 2005.

11 "Weasel-Words Rip My Flesh!" Jack Shafer. *Slate.* September 20, 2005.

12 "Working Moms Trying to Do It All May Be More Depressed." MSNBC. August 24, 2011.

13 "10 Secrets to Being Happy." Inara Verzemnieks. *Working Mother.* August 2011.

14 "Why Are Women So Unhappy At Work." Sean Silverthorne. CBS News. October 7, 2009.

15 "Blue Is the New Black." Maureen Dowd. *New York Times.* September 19, 2009.

16 "Liberated and Unhappy." Ross Douthat. *New York Times.* May 25, 2009.

17 Stein, Jeannine. "Does Working Make Mothers Happier and Healthier?" *LA Times.* December 13, 2011.

18 "Working Moms Feel Better than Stay-at-Home Moms, Study Finds." American Psychological Association. December 12, 2011.

19 Williams, Joan. "Opt Out' or Pushed Out?: How the Press Covers Work/Family Conflict." Work Life Law. 2006. http://www.worklifelaw.org/pubs/OptOutPushedOut.pdf

20 "Census Dispels 'Opting-Out' Notion for Stay-at-Home Moms." Donna St. George. *The Washington Post.* October 1, 2009.

Bibliography

Badinter, Élisabeth. *How Modern Motherhood Undermines the Status of Women.* Metropolitan Books, April 24, 2012.

Badinter, Élisabeth. *Mother Love: Myth and Reality.* Macmillan, 1981.

Block, Jennifer. *Pushed: The Painful Truth about Childbirth and Modern Maternity Care.* Da Capo Press, April 8, 2008.

Crittenden, Ann. *The Price of Motherhood: Why the Most Important Job in the World Is Still the Least Valued.* Picador, November 23, 2010.

Faludi, Susan. *Backlash: The Undeclared War Against American Women.* Broadway, August 15, 2006.

Flanagan, Caitlin. *To Hell With All That: Loving and Loathing Our Inner Housewife.* Back Bay Books, May 8, 2007.

Fey, Tina. *Bossypants.* Hachette Book Group, April 5, 2011.

Friedan, Betty. *The Feminine Mystique.* W. W. Norton & Company, September 17, 2001.

Gross-Loh, Christine. *The Diaper-Free Baby: The Natural Toilet Training Alternative.* William Morrow Paperbacks, January 2, 2007.

Hewlett, Sylvia Ann. *Creating a Life: Professional Women and the Quest for Children.* Mirimax, April 10, 2002.

Hirshman, Linda. *Get to Work . . . and Get a Life Before It's Too Late.* Penguin, May 29, 2007.

Hochschild, Arlie Russell. *The Second Shift: Working Parents and the Revolution at Home.* Piatkus Books, October 1990.

Kukla, Rebecca. *Mass Hysteria: Medicine, Culture, and Mothers' Bodies.* Rowman & Littlefield Publishers, October 4, 2005.

Ladd-Taylor, Molly, and Lauri Umansky. *"Bad" Mothers: The Politics of Blame in Twentieth-Century America.* NYU Press, January 1, 1998.

Mnookin, Seth. *The Panic Virus: The True Story Behind the Vaccine-Autism Controversy.* Simon & Schuster. January 3, 2012.

Murkoff, Heidi. *What to Expect When You're Expecting.* Workman Publishing Company, April 1, 2002.

Rivers, Caryl. *Selling Anxiety: How the News Media Scare Women.* UPNE, August 29, 2008.

Scott, Laura. *Two is Enough: A Couple's Guide to Living Childless by Choice.* Seal Press, September 22, 2009.

Schlessinger, Laura. *In Praise of Stay-at-Home Moms.* Harper, 2009.

Sears, William. *The Baby Book: Everything You Need to Know About Your Baby from Birth to Age Two.* Little, Brown and Company, March 2003.

Stearns, Peter. *Anxious Parents: A History of Modern Childrearing in America.* NYU Press, November 1, 2004.

Warner, Judith. *Perfect Madness.* Riverhead, February 7, 2006.

Wolf, Joan. *Is Breast Best? Taking on the Breastfeeding Experts and the New High Stakes of Motherhood.* NYU Press, December 19, 2010.

About the Author

JESSICA VALENTI IS the author of three previous books, including *The Purity Myth: How America's Obsession with Virginity Is Hurting Young Women.* She is editor of the award-winning anthology *Yes Means Yes: Visions of Female Sexual Power and a World Without Rape* and the founder of Feministing.com, which *Columbia Journalism Review* calls "head and shoulders above almost any writing on women's issues in mainstream media." She was the recipient of the Hillman Journalism Prize and was called one of the Top 100 Inspiring Women in the world by *The Guardian.* Jessica is a frequent contributor to *The Nation* and *The Washington Post,* among other publications. She lives with her family in Boston, but remains a New Yorker at heart.